The Heart Healthy Queen's Cookbook

137 Easy and Great-Tasting Recipes

All the best,
Cindy Stratioti

Cindy Stratioti

IN MEMORY

In loving memory of my dear mom, Betty Cran Berg.
Thanks for always encouraging me, supporting me,
believing in me, and loving me. I miss you so much.

DEDICATION

This cookbook is dedicated to my loving husband and best friend, Jeff. You are my inspiration. I am so proud of you and all that you have accomplished. I love you and your healthy heart!

ACKNOWLEDGEMENT

We extend our heartfelt appreciation to Essentia Health
St. Mary's Heart and Vascular Center, with special thanks and
acknowledgment to the Cardiac Rehab team. Thank you for your
professional care and concern during Jeff's recovery process
and ongoing journey. Your dedication, support and perspective
have been paramount in making our lifestyle changes. We are
forever grateful for everything you did and continue to do to
keep us heart healthy. Bless all of you.

CONTENTS

In Memory iii

Dedication v

Acknowledgement vii

Introduction and Our Story xi

Tips for Success That Worked for Us xv

In Our Opinion...Try These Spices and/or Brands xvii

Watching the Sodium: Easy Ways to Eat Better xxi

THE RECIPES 1

    Just for Starters 3

    The Smell of Good Bread Baking 13

Bread Making (Bread Machine Recipes) 15

    Quick Breads 21

    Bountiful Breakfasts 27

    Sprinkle Liberally with Condiments 37

    Use Your Spoon: Sustaining Soups And Stews 45

    Toss Me A Salad 65

    Make It A Savory Side 75

    Gather Around the Dinner Table 89

Sweet Endings 149

INDEX OF RECIPES **189**

About The Author 197

INTRODUCTION AND OUR STORY

Our eating habits changed December 12, 2010. It wasn't that we ate all the *wrong* things before that time; we just didn't pay such close attention. Attention to portion size, refined sugar, saturated fat and sodium just weren't on our radar.

But back to December 12th....actually December 11th. That's the day we were celebrating with good friends. Our Alma Mater, the UMD Bulldogs, won the semifinal football game and would travel to the Division II Finals in Florence, Alabama. We were enjoying a spicy pizza and a couple of beers at a local restaurant, savoring the victory and making plans to travel to Alabama. Jeff, my spouse, was a bit quiet, but nothing out of the ordinary. He rubbed his left arm a bit, but attributed the pain to a pulled muscle, and his chest discomfort to indigestion. We went home and went to bed. In hindsight, we were extremely lucky. That's an understatement.

The next morning, Jeff's coloring wasn't so great. I was reading the paper, drinking my coffee. I made a couple of comments to Jeff....."Are you feeling OK? Your coloring doesn't look so great." "No, I'm OK; I think I just pulled a muscle," he said. I went back to my coffee and paper. Being persistent, I inquired again. And to make a long story short, we ended up at the emergency room – Jeff presenting himself with left arm pain and some mild but constant chest pain. A few tests later the ER doctor confirmed "something going on with the heart." Cath lab and two stents later, the blockage was opened.....Jeff had had a heart attack at age 55. We were shocked, but relieved the blockage was addressed. It brought back tough memories of a date and time some 31 years before. We were newlyweds. My dad suffered a massive heart attack at age 55, and tragically and sadly didn't survive. It was the same time of year, so close to the holidays. Déjà vu all over again. But this time....a different outcome.

It wasn't long before Jeff started Cardiac Rehab. At a number of follow up appointments, we talked with nutritionists, psychologists, and a host of other health care professionals who helped map the recovery process. They talked to me, too, because "a heart attack affects the entire family." Ain't that the truth.

Jeff worked hard in his road to recovery. He watched cholesterol and blood pressure numbers, and closely followed a strict diet low in saturated fat and sodium. Still does. He greatly reduced his sugar intake (high triglycerides and sugar intake can go hand in hand). Jeff created a rigorous exercise schedule for himself and to this day, rarely wavers from it. By mid-March, 2011, results of a stress echo were excellent and Jeff was cleared to participate in competitive sports. That letter from Dr. Chiu still hangs on the refrigerator. And in 2013, Jeff was awarded the American Heart Associations "Lifestyle Change Award" for making outstanding lifestyle improvements to live a longer, stronger life.

So that's what Jeff did. What did I do to help support his recovery process? I had recently retired – after working 31 years in court administration. A life-long learner, I immersed myself in recipes – researching, analyzing, and experimenting. I learned most of our previous tried and true recipes had way too much saturated fat and sodium. No more pepperoni. No more casseroles with "cream of something" soup. Store bought jars of barbecue sauce, soy sauce and other condiments had sky-high sodium levels. I learned to make my own, and I started to cook differently. I donated a number of old cookbooks and modified recipes in those I kept.

We scoured labels. Grocery shopping became a "bingo" of sorts to find the lowest sodium, lowest saturated fat foods. Early on, grocery shopping took hours trying to find the "right" can of tomatoes or barbecue sauce. Shopping at the Whole Foods Co-op/Market and Trader Joe's provided us with a variety of tasty heart healthy options. I also found that, when I could, it was better to "make my own." I now had a new job....I dubbed myself the

"Heart Healthy Queen." It's good to be queen! And so started the journey to our lifestyle changes.

Oh sure, I had a few "food failures," but I had so many more successes. The low fat macaroni and cheese was particularly awful! Mac and cheese isn't meant to be low fat, I guess! In my recipes, I substituted new (and old) spices and flavored vinegars. As family and friends tasted the new or modified creations, they often asked for recipes. I was pleasantly surprised. The cookbook idea was hatched.

Recipes were accumulated from all over and represent the flavors we enjoy. Some are from friends, many were Mom's or from other relatives. Some I made up. I searched the Internet and bookmarked a number of excellent heart healthy sites. Jeff brought home recipes from the nutritionists at Essentia Health.

Following a low sodium, low fat, and low sugar diet and with increased exercise, Jeff lost 30 pounds. I lost ten. (Why is it so much easier for guys to lose weight?!?!? Sorry, I digress!)

The journey from 'not paying much attention' to diet to a heart healthy diet took some adjusting, but is a way of life for us now. What do we eat? We eat much of what we ate before, but we make better choices. You will find many of the recipes here. We follow the "diet" 9 days out of 10, give or take. On the day(s) we splurge, we get 'back on the wagon' the next day. We both feel better.

In the following pages you will find new recipes as well as lower fat and sodium versions of some old favorites, a number of slimmed down picks, and okay, maybe more than a few splurges. Tasty recipes, I promise! Nothing is too fancy or exotic; I expect you'll have most recipe ingredients already in your refrigerator or pantry. All recipes from other sources have been modified to not only reduce fat and sodium using healthier alternatives, but to enhance taste. Here's wishing you a delicious and healthy life! Enjoy!

P.S. I am not a medical professional. I am not a nutritionist. But I am passionate about healthy cooking and healthy eating.

Any comments or suggestions made in this cookbook are simply that: *suggestions for healthier alternatives.* Please take them in the spirit they are intended. And as always, if you have any questions about your own health, please contact your health care professional.

P.S.S. Calorie, sodium, and fat contents have been calculated to the best of my ability, and may be approximate. All recipes have been made with low sodium ingredients when available. Calculations have been made using the lowest sodium alternative.

TIPS FOR SUCCESS THAT WORKED FOR US

- Watch portion size....Portions are smaller than you think!
- Read, read, read the labels – the amount of sodium can vary tremendously.
- Sodium goal: 1500 mg per day. We generally have much less than this.
- Goal: Keep saturated fat at 2 or 3 grams per serving.
- Watch empty calories. They add up quickly.
- Avoid soda and high calorie drinks. They are high in sugar.
- Limit alcohol, but enjoy red wine now and then!
- Eat "clean." Stay away from high processed foods whenever possible.
- Choose lean cuts of meat; limit red meat, purchase cuts with the words "round" or "loin."
- Goal for snacks: Limit 2 per day; no more than 100 calories for each snack.
- Watch sugar – triglycerides can be raised by sugar.
- Cocoa helps a sweet tooth – and is better for you than regular chocolate.
- When you absolutely have to have chocolate, make it DARK!
- Eat unsalted nuts, but watch serving size. There are lots of calories in nuts.
- Go out for dinner once in a while, but make good choices – have an entrée that is broiled or grilled, watch the seasonings and ask for lower fat dressings or gravies on the side.
- When you "fall off the wagon" and have a "bad eating day," don't beat yourself up. Just get back on track the next day.
- Exercise more and eat less.
- Use common sense.

IN OUR OPINION...TRY THESE SPICES and/or BRANDS

Take a road trip to **Trader Joe's.** There are currently a number of stores in the Twin Cities (MN) metro area. Trader Joe's has an abundance of no salt and low sodium foods from soups to nuts! To determine if there is a location near you, www.traderjoes.com/stores.

Whole Foods Co-op/Market has a variety of low sodium staples and heart healthy options. Many items can be purchased in bulk.

Mrs. Dash seasonings and marinades. We especially like the tomato, basil, garlic blend. Others are also quite tasty.

Penzey's Spices have a good number of salt free spices. Penzey's brick and mortar stores are located in Milwaukee, WI and in the Twin Cities, or order from their catalog or online, www.penzeys.com.

Flavored vinegars and olive oils are available in grocery stores as well as specialty stores (and locally in the Duluth, MN area at The Rustic Olive, www.TheRusticOliveDuluth.com).

No or Low Sodium Broths/Bouillon: Herb Ox Sodium free (chicken or beef) Bouillon, Orrington Farms Broth Base and Seasoning, Swanson Unsalted Cooking Stock (chicken or beef), Imagine (Beef, Chicken or Vegetable) Flavored Broth – Low Fat, Low Sodium.

No Salt Added Tomato-Based Products: National brands such as Del Monte or Hunts Diced Tomatoes, or Hunts Tomato

Sauce, or check the "generic" brand at your store. Often, generic products are lowest in sodium content. Enrico's Pizza Sauce and Francesco Rinaldi Traditional Pasta Sauce are low in sodium and are our favorites. If you feel the need for more "zip," add some no-salt seasonings.

Fish: Tuna - StarKist Selects Very Low Sodium, Chunk White Albacore. Fresh salmon or frozen salmon burgers. (Fish is very good for a heart healthy diet. Unfortunately, Jeff is not a "fish guy").

Low Fat/Low Sodium Tub Margarine: Tub margarine is a better alternative than stick margarine. We use Canola Harvest and find it to be a good "butter spread" alternative. When you must use butter in recipes, choose unsalted or lower fat.

Beans: Canned beans are high in sodium. Best lower sodium products include Wild Harvest Organic or S&W Premium. (Black Beans or Kidney Beans). Or buy dried (packaged) beans, and soak you own.

Schwan's (distributed out of Marshall, MN) has a variety of yummy vegetables: Fire Roasted Blend, Mediterranean Blend, Roasted Peppers and Onions are our favorites. Try 'em, you'll like 'em! Check out their website at www.schwans.com or toll free 1-888-SCHWANS.

Cheese: Most cheese is way too high in saturated fat. Swiss cheese is lowest in fat and sodium. So we use Swiss, or a smaller amount of reduced fat mozzarella or cheddar. Sargento has a shredded Parmesan cheese that is only one gram of saturated fat and 60 mg of sodium. Fat free Ricotta cheese is also rather tasty. Cottage cheese is quite high in sodium. We eat it occasionally. There is a Fiber One cottage cheese that has reasonable sodium levels.

Try the Lower Cholesterol, Lower Sodium, Lower Fat Alternatives: Instead of eggs, try egg substitute (found in the refrigerated section of your grocery store). Replace full fat cream cheese with fat free cream cheese (or at least low fat). Little adjustments can make a big difference.

Keep in mind that your choice of bread, canned item, jarred sauce, etc. can vary *tremendously* in sodium content. Always look for the lowest sodium, lowest fat alternative.

WATCHING THE SODIUM:
EASY WAYS TO EAT BETTER

- Remove the salt shaker from the kitchen table. Stop adding salt to your food.
- Pick foods naturally low in sodium. Fresh is best. Stock up in the produce aisle. Choose fruits and vegetables in season. Low fat milk, olive oil, yogurt, fish and pasta are all good choices.
- Learn to read food labels. Look for foods labeled low sodium, reduced sodium, or no salt added.
- Adapt your preferred foods to low sodium versions. Whatever your palate, there are many no-salt seasonings and flavorings available.
- Eating at home gives you control of what you put on your plate.
- Share your low sodium lifestyle with family and friends. You will all eat better!
- Make good choices.

MAKE YOUR OWN!!

Really, it is not hard to make your own sauces or condiments, and it is much healthier – you can control the levels of sodium and fat. Check the short section on condiments that follows.

EXPERIMENT!!

I generally make a recipe "as written" the first time I try it. After that I adapt the recipe to our tastes. Feel free to experiment and add more or less of a spice, adjust, and make it your own. When you get lots of raves for a particular recipe you adjusted, just re-member to write it down so you can make it the same way the next time (she says with experience)! I am constantly finding new recipes to try, and Jeff is generally a willing guinea pig! And it keeps meal time interesting!

SPICE IS NICE

Many people tell me food is bland without salt. I respectfully disagree. Salt is an acquired taste. Go for the flavor, and spice it up! Flavor your food with no-salt-added spices. Use flavored vinegars and olive oils, oregano, basil and other no-salt Italian seasonings, cumin, chili or red pepper for heat, lemon pepper, or other favorite no-salt blends. The seasonings are endless and the results can be amazing! Read the labels to be sure your favorite spice is really salt free.

OK TO SPLURGE ONCE IN A WHILE

Yes, it's okay to splurge once in a while, just don't make a habit out of it. I am of the opinion that if you are too rigid in your eating, you can slip back to bad habits, because your taste buds "miss" some of what they experienced previously. So, when the splurge occurs, simply "readjust." Make up for it with something extra healthy for your other meals. When you're on vacation, don't overly stress about meals. Eat smart, drink smart, exercise if you can, and walk, walk, walk. Then get back to your healthy lifestyle when you return from your travels. I am a big believer in "most everything in moderation." The key word is moderation.

THE RECIPES

Just for Starters

FAT FREE DILL DIP

An easy-to-put-together, good vegetable dip.

1 c. fat free sour cream
1 c. fat free mayonnaise
1 T. parsley flakes
1 T. dried minced onion
1 T. dill weed
¼ t. garlic powder

Combine all ingredients; chill at least 1 hour.

Per 2 T. serving = 65 calories, 0 fat, 0 cholesterol, 190 mg sodium

GRAPE TOMATO BRUSCHETTA

Bruschetta is one of our favorite appetizers to order out. Here's one to make at home. Top with a bit of grated mozzarella or Parmesan cheese if you like.

3 pints grape tomatoes
1 T. olive oil
3 cloves garlic, minced
1/8 t. salt
½ t. black pepper
¼ t. Mrs. Dash tomato basil garlic seasoning
¼ c. fresh basil
1 T. red wine vinegar
14 slices toasted, thinly-sliced baguette
Additional fresh basil for garnish
Parmesan or mozzarella cheese, optional

Preheat oven to 325 degrees. Toss tomatoes with oil, garlic, salt, pepper and Mrs. Dash seasoning. Place tomato mixture on baking sheet and roast until broken down, about 40 minutes. Combine roasted tomatoes with fresh basil and vinegar. Top baguette slices with tomato mixture. Garnish with fresh basil and add a bit of grated Parmesan or mozzarella cheese if desired. Place under broiler for a minute or two to "crisp up."

Per 1 slice serving = 69 calories, 0 g saturated fat, 0 cholesterol, 178 mg sodium

5

GUACAMOLE

This one came from my sister and brother-in-law. It is so easy to make, is very low in sodium, plus has an added bonus: avocado has lots of "good" (not saturated) fat.

1 avocado, peeled, pitted and mashed
The juice of one lime
¼ to ½ c. diced onion
1 or 2 Roma tomatoes, diced
1 t. minced garlic
¼ t. white pepper
1 T. fresh cilantro (or 1 t. dried), optional
1 pinch cayenne pepper (optional)

Combine all ingredients. Cover and refrigerate for 1 hour to allow flavor to develop.

Yield: 4 servings

Per serving = 55 calories, 1 g saturated fat, 0 mg cholesterol, 4 mg sodium

KEY LIME DIP

Thread chunks of fruit onto bamboo skewers and enjoy this yummy dip.

8 oz. fat free key lime yogurt
1 ½ c. fat free cream cheese
2 T. powdered sugar
1 t. coconut extract
¼ t. almond extract

Combine ingredients; beat with mixer at medium speed until smooth.

Chill. Serve with pineapple, whole strawberries, kiwi, melons, etc.

Per serving with 2 fruit skewers and 1/3 c. dip = 151 calories, 0.5 g saturated fat, 6 mg cholesterol, 40 mg sodium

PARTY CRUNCH MIX

Some days you just need "crunch!" Tasty party mix is better to eat than high-fat potato chips. A touch of heat comes through in this blend of cereals, pretzels and bagel chips, and Italian seasonings and Parmesan cheese boost the flavor in this snack mix. Best of all, it's microwaved!

1 ½ c. Corn Chex
1 ½ c. Rice Chex
1 ½ c. Wheat Chex
½ c. low sodium bagel chips
½ c. mini (unsalted) pretzels
3 T. unsalted butter, melted
½ t. garlic powder
½ t. basil
½ t. oregano
¼ t. red pepper flakes
¼ t. onion powder
2 T. Parmesan cheese

In a large microwave-safe bowl, combine cereals, chips and pretzels. In small bowl, combine butter and seasonings; pour over cereal and toss to coat.

Microwave uncovered on high for 2 minutes, stirring once. Stir in Parmesan cheese. Cook 4 minutes longer, stirring twice. Spread onto waxed paper to cool. Store in air tight container.

Per ½ c. serving = 80 calories, 2 g saturated fat, 8 mg cholesterol, 125 mg sodium

TORTILLA ROLL UPS

I adapted this recipe from an old "Pine to Prairie" cookbook (Telephone Pioneers of America). It's yummy!

3 oz. fat free cream cheese
8 oz. fat free sour cream
1 (4 oz) can green chilies, chopped
2 c. reduced fat shredded cheddar cheese
¼ t. garlic powder
2 or 3 shakes of Tabasco sauce
1 pkg. white corn tortillas or the lowest sodium flour tortillas you can find.

Mix ingredients together and spread mixture on the tortillas. Roll tight and wrap in plastic wrap. Chill overnight. Slice and serve with low sodium salsa.

Per 3 slice serving = 65 calories, 2 g fat, 20 mg cholesterol, 138 mg sodium

VANILLA WALNUT CRUNCHIES

Walnuts are a great source of Omega-3s, and these walnuts are delicious! Just remember to stir them occasionally while they are baking, and watch them carefully so they don't burn!

1/3 c. sugar
¼ t. salt
¼ t. coriander
¼ t. cinnamon
¼ t. allspice
¼ t. nutmeg
1/8 t. pepper
4 c. walnut halves
2 T. canola oil
1 T. vanilla extract
¼ t. almond extract

In a bowl, combine all ingredients except walnuts, oil and extracts. In a large bowl, combine walnuts, oil and extracts. Add sugar mixture to walnut mixture; toss to coat.

Transfer to a large jelly roll pan that has been lined with aluminum foil and the foil coated with cooking spray. Bake at 325 degrees for 25 to 30 minutes, stirring occasionally. Cool completely and store in airtight container....if they last that long!

Per 1/3 c. serving = 243 calories, 22 g fat, 2 g saturated fat, 0 cholesterol, 46 mg sodium

VEGGIE PINWHEEL APPETIZERS

Easy to make ahead of time. Easy to serve. Serve with low sodium salsa.

8 oz. reduced fat cream cheese
2 T. low sodium Vidalia onion salad dressing
½ c. finely chopped broccoli
½ c. finely chopped cauliflower
¼ c. grated carrot
¼ c. finely chopped red onion
½ t. dill weed
2 drops Tabasco sauce
4 whole wheat tortillas

Beat cream cheese and salad dressing in a bowl until blended. Stir in vegetables, dill weed and Tabasco sauce. Spread over tortillas. Roll up tightly and wrap in plastic wrap. Refrigerate overnight, or for at least 2 hours before serving. Unwrap; cut into slices.

Per 2 slice serving = 40 calories 2 g fat, 1 g saturated fat, 5 mg cholesterol, 56 mg sodium

VEGGIE PIZZA

Son Peter's favorite appetizer. And a hit every time I make it!

2 packages reduced fat crescent rolls
8 oz. fat free cream cheese
1 c. fat free sour cream
¾ c. low fat mayonnaise
1 ½ T. "Hidden Valley" Dressing mix (recipe follows in condiment section, page 38)
Reduced fat cheddar or Swiss cheese
Small pieces of your favorite vegetables: cauliflower, carrots, broccoli, green pepper, tomato, etc.

Place rolls flat on jelly roll pan, pinch seams together; bake as directed on package, about 10 minutes.   Mix cream cheese, sour cream, mayonnaise and "Hidden Valley" Dressing mix, and spread mixture on top of cooled rolls. Sprinkle with vegetables and cheese. Refrigerate until ready to serve.

Yield: 12 generous servings.

Per Serving = 65 calories, 3 g fat, 30 mg cholesterol, 135 mg sodium

The Smell of Good Bread Baking

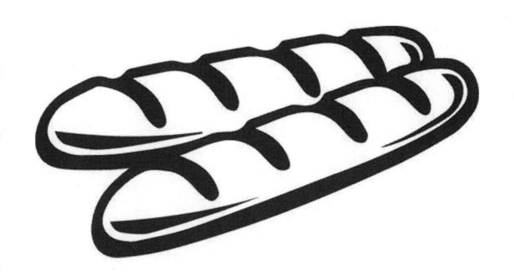

BREAD MAKING
(BREAD MACHINE RECIPES)

There are many rewards of baking your own bread. First and foremost, the kitchen smells so wonderful when bread is baking. Second, nothing beats the flavor of homemade bread. Third, you get to control the amount of sodium in your bread. And finally, making bread in a bread machine is very easy!

Store bought and bakery bread typically has 150 to 220 mg per serving. The yeast-bread recipes that follow are single digit sodium. Many of the bread recipes were found online while researching low sodium bread recipes.

One issue I have had with salt-free bread making is that I more than occasionally find that the loaf collapses on top when I open the bread machine. When the bread machine beeps "I'm done," I ever-so-carefully open the top of the machine and peer in. Success? Oh, maybe 65 percent of the time!

After some research, I now understand that a cause of collapsing bread is *because* there is no salt in the recipe (salt apparently controls the speed of yeast). Another cause is the *type* of bread machine. Apparently machines like mine that are *vertical* have more collapsing problems with salt free recipes. I may need to invest in a new machine (that's a hint, Jeff!).

Still, I persevere! I have some success with a number of different breads including white, honey wheat, multigrain, and French and Italian breads. And if they collapse, we eat them anyway! They still taste great.

P.S. In my research for this cookbook, I have since learned that when bread collapses, a fix is to reduce the amount of yeast or reduce the liquid by a tablespoon or two. So I will keep experimenting. . . And practice makes perfect....sometimes!

EXTRAORDINARY WHITE BREAD

Hard to peg something as "extraordinary," but for a low sodium bread, this is really good.

1 c. + 2 T. warm water
1 ½ T. unsalted butter
3 c. bread flour (all-purpose works too)
2 rounded T. nonfat dry milk powder
2 T. sugar
1 ½ t. yeast

Add ingredients to bread machine pan in the order above. Select basic/white bread cycle, medium/normal color setting.

Yield: 12 slices

Per 1 slice serving = 148 calories, 2 g fat, 1 g saturated fat, 4 mg cholesterol, 6 mg sodium

FRENCH BREAD

This recipe can be processed in a bread machine on either white or French cycle. If you are strapped for time, the white cycle works just fine. Also tastes good.

1 ½ c. warm water
2 t. unsalted butter
4 c. bread flour (or all-purpose flour)
4 t. sugar
1 ¼ t. yeast

Place ingredients in bread machine in order above. Process on white or French cycle.

Yield: 12 servings

Per 1 slice serving = 175 calories, 1 g saturated fat, 2 mg cholesterol, 2 mg sodium

HONEY WHEAT BREAD

Wheat breads take a good hour longer to make, at least in my bread machine. Plan accordingly. Honey provides a subtle, sweet flavor in this low sodium bread.

1 c. plus 2 T. warm water
1 ½ T. unsalted butter
¼ c. honey
1 ½ c. bread flour
1 ½ c. whole wheat flour
1 T. nonfat dry milk powder
1 t. yeast

Place ingredients in bread machine pan in above order. Process on whole wheat cycle.

Yield: 12 servings

Per 1 slice serving = 149 calories, 2 g fat, 1 g saturated fat, 4 mg cholesterol, 4 mg sodium

ITALIAN BREAD

This is a tasty bread for dipping in olive oil. It also pairs nicely with minestrone or other hearty soups.

3 T. extra virgin olive oil (or use flavored olive oil such as basil, Tuscan Herb, etc.)
1 c. warm water
3 c. bread flour
1 ½ t. yeast

Place in bread machine in order above. Process on white or French bread cycle.

Yield: 12 servings

Per 1 slice serving = 155 calories, 4 g fat, 1 g saturated fat, 0 mg cholesterol, 1 mg sodium

MULTIGRAIN BREAD

This is probably my favorite bread machine recipe. It's a bit dense, but is quite flavorful. You can find seven grain cereal in the bulk section of your grocery store, or at a Whole Foods Store. If you can't find seven grain cereal, a five grain can be substituted without any issue.

1 c. plus 2 T. warm water
2 T. unsalted butter
1 1/3 c. bread flour
1 c. whole wheat flour
¼ c. seven-grain cereal
3 T. light brown sugar
2 ¼ t. yeast

Place ingredients in bread machine in order as above. Process on whole wheat cycle.

Yield: 12 servings

Per 1 slice serving = 128 calories, 2 g fat, 1 g saturated fat, 5 mg cholesterol, 4 mg sodium

Quick Breads

BANANA OATMEAL BREAD

This banana bread is heavier than most and perhaps more suitable for breakfast. Orange zest, oatmeal and oat bran add to the heartiness of this bread. Add 1/3 cup of dark chocolate chips in place of the dried fruit for a nice change, or gently fold in 1/3 cup of raspberries before baking.

¾ c. fat free or low fat milk
½ c. quick cooking oatmeal
½ c. brown sugar
1 or 2 bananas, mashed
½ c. dried fruit (raisins, cranberries, apricots, dates), optional
1 egg or equivalent egg substitute
2 T. canola oil
2 ¼ t. grated orange zest
1 c. all-purpose flour
½ c. whole wheat flour
½ c. oat bran
2. t. baking powder
¼ t. baking soda
1 ½ t. cinnamon
½ t nutmeg
Chopped nuts, if desired

Preheat oven to 350 degrees and spray a large loaf pan with nonstick spray.

In a medium bowl, stir together milk, oatmeal, brown sugar, bananas, dried fruit (if desired), egg or egg substitute, oil and orange zest. Stir remaining ingredients in another bowl. Add to milk mixture, and stir until moistened. Don't over mix.

Pour batter into prepared loaf pan. Bake 45 minutes or until a toothpick inserted in center comes out clean. Invert bread onto a cooling rack to cool.

Yield: 12 servings

Per 1 slice serving = 113 calories, 2 g fat, 0 saturated fat, 0 mg cholesterol, 98 mg sodium

CHOCOLATE CHIP BANANA BREAD

Here is yet another banana bread recipe, and no mixer is needed for this one. Recipe was adapted from a low salt cookbook of the American Heart Association.

1 c. all-purpose flour
¾ c. whole wheat flour
2/3 c. sugar or Splenda
1/3 c. dark chocolate chips
2 t. baking powder
½ t. cinnamon
1/8 t. nutmeg
1 or 2 mashed, ripe bananas
1/3 c. unsweetened applesauce
1 large egg or equivalent egg substitute
1 T. canola oil

Preheat oven to 350 degrees. Lightly spray a large loaf pan with nonstick baking spray.

In a large bowl, stir together flour, sugar or Splenda, chocolate chips, baking powder, cinnamon and nutmeg. Make a well in the center. Add remaining ingredients; stir until just moistened. Don't over mix. Batter should be lumpy. Pour into loaf pan. Bake for 55 minutes or until a toothpick inserted in center comes out clean. Invert bread onto cooling rack to cool.

Yield: 12 servings

Per 1 slice serving = 130 calories, 2 g fat, 1 g saturated fat, 0 cholesterol, 74 mg sodium

HANNAH'S BANANA BREAD

Do you have some ripe bananas? A delicious and moist bread, this was my maternal grandma's recipe. Pump up your potassium, and have a slice!

½ c. unsalted butter
1 c. sugar (or combination of sugar and Splenda)
2 eggs or equivalent egg substitute
2 bananas
2 c. flour (or combination of all purpose and whole wheat flour)
1 t. soda
½ t. salt
Optional: chopped walnuts

Cream shortening, add sugar, and add beaten eggs or egg substitute and bananas. Stir in dry ingredients, and beat well. Pour in bread pan that has been prepared with nonstick baking spray. Bake in a 350 degree oven for 1 to 1 ¼ hours or until toothpick inserted in center comes out clean.

Yield: 12 servings

Per 1 slice serving = 200 calories, 2.5 g saturated fat, 20 mg cholesterol, 137 mg sodium

LOW FAT LEMON BLUEBERRY LOAF

I love anything lemon. Jeff loves blueberries—hence this lemon blueberry loaf. Yummy!

¼ c. canola oil
2 T. lemon juice
1 egg plus 2 egg whites
½ c. low or fat free milk
1 ½ c. flour
2. t. baking powder
¾ c. sugar or Splenda
¼ t. salt
1 T. lemon zest
1 c. blueberries

Combine oil, lemon juice, eggs, and milk in small bowl. Place dry ingredients in a large bowl; mix. Make a well in dry ingredients. Add wet to dry ingredients, and stir until just moistened. Fold in blueberries. Bake at 350 degrees for one hour or until toothpick inserted in center comes out clean.

Yield: 12 servings

Per 1 slice serving = 185 calories, 2 g fat, 22 mg cholesterol, 102 mg sodium

Bountiful Breakfasts

APPLE PANCAKES

Applesauce gives these pancakes a good flavor. This recipe makes 6 servings, so at least double it if you are feeding a crew.

1 c. all purpose flour
½ c. whole wheat flour
1 T. baking powder
2 T. sugar
¼ t. nutmeg
2 large eggs
1 c. low fat milk
1 c. applesauce
2 T. unsalted butter, melted

Combine dry ingredients in large bowl. Make a well in the center of the ingredients in the bowl. Add eggs, milk, applesauce and melted butter. Stir together until mixtures are blended, but still lumpy. Heat and grease griddle and pour ¼ c. onto griddle for each pancake. Cook until browned on bottom, then flip and cook other side.

Yield: 6 servings

Per serving (2 or 3 pancakes) = 244 calories, 1 g saturated fat, 83 mg cholesterol, 70 mg sodium

BREAKFAST SAUSAGE

This recipe was borrowed from Essentia's Cardiac Rehab Center and was adapted from the Biggest Loser Cookbook. I turned down the heat a bit.

½ pound ground extra lean pork or turkey
2 T. finely chopped onion
½ t. garlic powder
½ t. thyme
¼ t. savory
1/8 t. cayenne
¼ t. pepper

Combine meat, onion, and spices in a mixing bowl. Mix ingredients well. Divide mixture into 4 equal parts. Shape each into a ball, and then flatten into a patty. Stack patties between sheets of waxed paper. If not cooking right away, store in airtight container and refrigerate for up to 3 days or freeze up to one month.

Cook over medium high heat in skillet misted with olive oil spray. Cook 2 minutes per side or until starting to brown and no longer pink inside.

Makes 4 patties.

Per patty = 72 calories, 2 g fat, saturated fat less than 1 g, 37 mg cholesterol, 101 mg sodium

BREAKFAST SCRAMBLE

Add other seasonal vegetables....And at our house, double the recipe!

1 T. basil olive oil
¼ c. onion, finely chopped
¼ c. red bell pepper, chopped
½ c. frozen hash browns
3 eggs or ¾ c. egg substitute

In large skillet prepared with nonstick cooking spray, sauté onion and red bell pepper in oil over medium heat. Add hash browns and cook until potatoes are softened and beginning to brown; stir occasionally. Whisk eggs or egg substitute until well blended. Pour over vegetables and cook until eggs are set, about 5 to 6 minutes, stirring occasionally.

Yield: 2 servings.

Per serving = 283 calories. With eggs = 3 g saturated fat. With egg substitute = 0 fat, 5 mg cholesterol, 136 mg sodium

BREAKFAST TACOS

This one is easy to make and is quite good. Add peppers and onions to get those veggies in.

8 corn taco shells
1 c. egg substitute or 8 eggs
¼ c. low sodium salsa
¼ c. reduced fat Swiss cheese

Scramble eggs, stirring in salsa and cheese when almost set. Divide into tacos, sitting them upright in baking dish. Microwave 1 minute or heat at 350 degrees for five minutes.

Yield: 8 servings

With egg substitute 2 tacos = 205 calories, 3 g saturated fat, 8 mg cholesterol, 125 mg sodium

MOM'S HOLIDAY BRUNCH

A tradition at our house is to make Mom's brunch for Christmas breakfast. These days, it is lightened up quite a bit. The Velveeta cheese and high fat sausage have been replaced with low fat cheese and breakfast sausage (see recipe on page 29) or the lowest fat and sodium sausage I can find at the grocery store.

Prepare sausage: Use breakfast sausage recipe, or use store-bought sausage. If sausage is not "pre- cooked," bake sausage on a jelly roll pan lined with several layers of paper towels to absorb grease, 20 minutes at 375 degrees.

Cube 8 slices of low sodium bread
Place in a 9x13 pan coated with nonstick cooking spray
Add 1 ½ c. low fat cheddar or Swiss cheese
8 eggs (or equivalent egg substitute)
Beat the eggs with 4 c. low fat milk
Add:
½ t. Mrs. Dash Original Blend seasoning
1/8 t. pepper
Pinch dry mustard

Pour egg mixture over bread and cheese mixture.

Place sausages on top of bread and egg mixture.

Cover pan with aluminum foil and refrigerate overnight. Bake one hour covered, then additional half hour uncovered in a 400 degree oven.

Yield: 8 servings

Per generous serving = 215 calories, 4 g fat, 35 mg cholesterol, 144 mg sodium

PANCAKES

Enjoy your morning with pancakes for breakfast. Don't over mix the batter, or pancakes become tough and chewy. This recipe was borrowed from our friends at the Cardiac Rehab Center at Essentia Health.

1 c. all-purpose flour
¼ c. whole wheat flour
2 T. sugar or sugar substitute
2 t. baking powder
1 large egg
1 c. low fat milk
1 T. cider vinegar
1 T. canola oil

Stir together dry ingredients. Add egg, milk, vinegar and oil to flour mixture and stir until blended but slightly lumpy. Pour ¼ cupfuls of batter onto hot greased griddle for each pancake. Cook until browned on bottom; turn and cook on other side until done.

Yield: 4 servings

Per serving (2 or 3 large pancakes) = 225 calories, 0.5 g saturated fat, 60 mg cholesterol, 300 mg sodium

(There is a sodium-free baking powder – Hain Baking Powder. If sodium-free baking powder is used, the sodium would decrease to 50 mg per serving).

VEGGIE EGG STRATA

Borrowed from the back of a Ry Krisp box!

9 Ry Krisp Light (or equivalent) crackers
8 oz. frozen roasted peppers and onions (or veggie blend of your choice)
1 cup reduced fat shredded mozzarella cheese
8 large eggs (or equivalent egg substitute)
¾ c. low fat or skim milk (we use 1%)
¼ t. pepper
¼ t. dried Italian seasoning (no salt)

Preheat oven to 350 degrees. Coat an 11x7 inch baking dish with nonstick cooking spray. Place crackers in the baking dish, breaking crackers if necessary to fit pan. Top with roasted peppers and onions, and shredded cheese. In a large bowl, whisk eggs, milk, pepper and Italian seasoning. Pour mixture over veggies.

Bake for one hour or until a knife inserted in center comes out clean. Let stand for 5 minutes before serving.

Yield: 6 servings

Per serving = 145 calories, 3.5 g saturated fat, 23 mg cholesterol, 202 mg sodium

WHOLE WHEAT WAFFLES

This recipe came from a Taste of Home insert. I modified it a bit to add some orange flavor.

2 eggs or ½ c. egg substitute
1¾ c. low fat milk
½ c. fat free vanilla or orange flavored yogurt
1 t. orange zest
1 T. vanilla
1 c. all-purpose flour
1 c. whole wheat flour
½ c. Splenda or appropriate sugar substitute
2 T. sugar
4 t. baking powder
1/8 t. salt

Beat eggs or egg substitute in large bowl. Add milk, yogurt, orange zest and vanilla; mix well. Combine flours, Splenda, sugar, baking powder and salt; stir into mixture until just combined. Bake in preheated waffle iron until golden brown.

Yield: 20 waffles (4 in. x 4 in.)

Per serving (2 waffles) = 137 calories. If using egg substitute, 1 g fat (trace saturated fat), 3 mg cholesterol, 185 mg sodium

Sprinkle Liberally with Condiments

"HIDDEN VALLEY" RANCH DRESSING MIX

I can't tell the difference between this homemade dressing mix and the packet at the grocery store.

½ c. dry buttermilk powder
1 T. parsley
1 t. minced onion
1 t. dill weed
1 t. onion powder
½ t. garlic powder
¼ t. pepper

Mix all together. Use 1 to 1 ½ T. in any recipe that calls for a packet of Hidden Valley Dressing mix. Store in refrigerator.

0 fat, 0 cholesterol, 32 mg sodium

LOW SODIUM BBQ SAUCE

A staple for grilling and to use in so many recipes, this BBQ sauce beats the grocery brand by leaps and bounds in the sodium category. Adjust seasonings to your own taste, or consider adding a bit of honey, molasses, a dash or more of Tabasco sauce, or your own ideas. This recipe adapted from Randy Van Horn and Essentia's Cardiac Rehab Center.

1 c. no sodium ketchup
2 (8 oz) cans no salt tomato sauce
1 (6 oz) can no salt tomato paste
1/3 c. apple cider vinegar
¼ c. light brown sugar
¼ c. Worcestershire sauce
¼ c. dry minced onion
1 T. chili powder
1 t. garlic powder
1 t. dry mustard
1 T. liquid smoke
¾ c. water

Combine all ingredients in a slow cooker. Heat on low for 4 to 6 hours.

Per 1 T. serving = 10 calories, 0 fat, 0 cholesterol, 12 mg sodium

REFRIGERATOR SWEET PICKLES

It's hard to find pickles that are salt-free, so might as well make your own. These pickles stay crisp because they aren't "cooked." Combine all the ingredients, add the cucumbers, and they will keep in refrigerator for up to 9 months. This adapted from a similar recipe from Essentia Health Cardiac Rehab Center.

2 c. sugar
2 c. white wine vinegar
1 ½ c. red wine vinegar
1 ½ c. cider vinegar
4 T. dill weed
1 t. black pepper
2 t. celery seed
½ t. dry mustard
½ t. turmeric
5 or 6 cucumbers

Combine all ingredients except cucumbers. Stir until sugar is dissolved. Put cucumbers in jars and pour the liquid over. Put lids on and store in refrigerator.

Yield: 32 servings

Per serving = 56 calories, 0 gm saturated fat, 0 mg cholesterol, 2 mg sodium

SOY SAUCE SUBSTITUTE

Soy sauce has sky-high levels of sodium. This substitute has only 5 mg of sodium and no fat. While it doesn't taste exactly like soy sauce, it is close enough for me. I found this recipe at cdkitchen.com.

2 T. sodium free beef bouillon or broth base
2 t. red wine vinegar
1 t. molasses
1/8 t. ginger
1/8 t. pepper
1/8 t. garlic powder
¾ c. water

Combine all ingredients; boil gently uncovered 5 minutes or until mixture is reduced to ½ c. Stir before using, and store in refrigerator.

Per 2 T. serving: 0 fat, 5 mg sodium

TACO SEASONING

Taco seasoning packets are notorious for being high in sodium. I expect you have these spices readily available in your pantry. This recipe makes enough for a meal of tacos, or double or triple the ingredients and keep it on hand. This recipe was adapted from one we obtained from the Cardiac Rehab Center at Essentia Health.

2 t. chili powder
½ t. onion powder
2 t. flour
1 t. cumin
2 t. oregano
½ t. garlic powder
½ t. cayenne OR crushed red pepper

Combine all ingredients in a small bowl and blend well. Makes a generous 2 T. of seasoning mix. Store in a cool, dry place. Use within 6 months.

To make taco filling: Brown 1 lb. extra lean ground beef or turkey in a skillet over medium high heat. Drain any grease. Add ½ to ¾ c. water and the seasoning mix. (2 T.) Reduce heat and simmer 10 minutes. Makes filling for approximately 8 tacos.

Per 2 T. Serving = 30 calories, 0 g saturated fat, 0 cholesterol, 5 mg sodium

EGG SUBSTITUTES

I have had limited success in utilizing egg substitutes. Sometimes the taste of an entrée changes, other times the substitution works just fine. While eggs are low in sodium and low in saturated fat (1.63 g), a standard egg has 186 mg cholesterol. So if you are watching your cholesterol, limiting eggs in your diet is a good thing.

HOMEMADE EGG SUBSTITUTE MIX

To replace one large egg:
2 T. flour + ½ t. canola oil + ½ t. baking powder + 2 T. liquid (low fat milk, diluted yogurt, soy milk, etc.)
OR
2 T. water + 1 T. oil + ½ t. baking powder. Beat together until smooth.

OTHER EGG SUBSTITUTES

1/3 c. applesauce = 1 egg
OR
¼ c. applesauce + 1 t. baking powder = 1 egg
OR
½ pureed banana (about ¼ c.) = 1 egg
OR
¼ c. canola oil = 1 egg
OR
1 T. cornstarch + 2 T. water = 1 egg
OR
1/3 c. cooked pumpkin = 1 egg
OR
Commercial egg beaters/egg white product

Use Your Spoon: Sustaining Soups And Stews

BEEF BARLEY SOUP

Stove top or slow cooker....whatever the approach, it tastes great!

1 lb. extra lean ground beef
1 large onion, chopped
1 c. shredded carrots
1 (14.5 oz) can low sodium beef (or vegetable) broth
4 c. water
2 T. low sodium beef bouillon
1 c. barley (quick cooking)
½ t. garlic powder
2 t. Worcestershire sauce
½ t. thyme

Brown ground beef and onion. Transfer to slow cooker, added remaining ingredients, and cook on low 6 to 8 hours.

Per 1 c. serving = 307 calories, 1.5 g saturated fat, 47 mg cholesterol, 102 mg sodium

CHICKEN BARLEY SOUP

This soup is chocked full of flavor.

1 lb. boneless skinless chicken breasts cut into small pieces
1 T. canola oil, or use olive oil cooking spray
1 medium onion, chopped
2 stalks of celery, chopped
2 or 3 carrots, sliced
32 oz. low sodium chicken broth
2 c. water
1 bay leaf
½ t. thyme
¼ t. pepper
½ t. garlic powder
½ c. quick cooking barley

In Dutch oven, brown chicken in oil or cooking spray. Remove chicken and set aside. In the same pan, sauté onion, celery and carrots for 3 to 4 minutes. Stir in broth, water, seasonings and chicken. Bring to a boil. Reduce to heat; cover and simmer for 20 minutes. Stir in barley and return to a boil. Reduce heat; cover and simmer for 10 to 12 minutes until barley and vegetables are tender. Discard bay leaf.

Per 1 c. serving = 218 calories, 1 g saturated fat, 42 mg cholesterol, 125 mg sodium

CHICKEN WILD RICE SOUP

This recipe came from Essentia Health's Cardiac Rehab Center with a tweak or two.

2 T. canola oil
½ c. chopped celery
8 oz. fresh mushrooms, sliced (optional)
2 c. cooked wild rice
½ t. dry mustard
3 T. dry white wine
2 c. fat free evaporated milk
1 lb. boneless chicken breast, cooked and cubed
4 c. low sodium chicken stock or broth
1 medium onion, chopped
1 c. carrots, sliced
2 T. flour
½ t. Penzey's Mural of Flavor (or substitute ¼ t. marjoram and ¼ t. thyme)
½ t. pepper

Add oil to Dutch oven, place over medium heat. Stir in onion, celery and carrots; sauté for 5 minutes. Add mushrooms, if desired and sauté for 2 more minutes. Add flour and stir well. Gradually pour in chicken broth, stirring constantly, until all has been added. Bring to a boil, reduce heat and let simmer. Add wild rice, chicken, spices, and wine. Heat through. Pour in evaporated milk. Let simmer for 1 hour.

Per 1 c. serving = 180 calories, 1 g saturated fat, 20 mg cholesterol, 200 mg sodium

CHILI

Who doesn't enjoy a bowl of zesty chili?

1 ½ lbs. extra lean ground beef or ground turkey
1 (15 oz) can no-salt added kidney beans
1 (15 oz) can no salt diced tomatoes
1 (8 oz) can no salt tomato sauce
1 medium onion, chopped
1 green pepper, chopped
1 (4 oz) can chopped green chilies
1 T. parsley
1 T. chili powder
¼ t. garlic powder
½ t. paprika
¼ t. pepper

Brown beef or turkey; drain fat. Add remaining ingredients. Simmer on stove top for 2 hours to blend seasonings.

Per 1 c. serving = 380 calories, 3 g saturated fat, 76 mg cholesterol, 120 mg sodium

CONDENSED CREAM OF MUSHROOM SOUP

Have you checked the sodium in canned soups? It's really high.
Use this in any recipes that call for "cream of something" soup.

1 c. sliced mushrooms
½ c. chopped onion
½ c. low sodium chicken broth
1 T. parsley
¼ t. garlic powder
2/3 c. non-fat, non-dairy creamer
2 T. cornstarch

Cook mushrooms, onions and spices in chicken broth until soft.
Process in blender/food processor until pureed. Shake together
creamer and cornstarch until dissolved. Cook and stir until
thick. Stir in vegetable mix.

Per 1 c. serving = 0 fat, 0 cholesterol, 18 mg sodium

CREAM SOUP MIX SUBSTITUTE

I keep this on hand in my pantry. It's a good alternative to "cream of something" soups. When making the soup, whisk in some chopped broccoli for 'cream of broccoli soup' or add some cooked and chopped chicken for 'cream of chicken soup.' A tablespoon of low sodium beef bouillon and some mushrooms makes 'cream of mushroom soup.' Or make it without any of the extras for an ordinary cream soup.

2 c. skim milk powder
1 c. cornstarch
¼ c. low sodium chicken bouillon
2 T. dried onion flakes
½ t. pepper

Combine all ingredients and store in airtight container.

To substitute for 1 can of soup, combine 1/3 c. mix and 1 ¼ c. water. Whisk well and cook over medium heat until thickened.

Per 'can' of soup = 0 fat, 0 cholesterol, 126 mg sodium

FAVORITE BROWN BEEF STEW

This is an old family staple. Didn't have to do anything to this one but get rid of the salt and use low sodium ketchup.

1 lb. appropriate beef (such as round steak), browned (trim fat)
¼ t. pepper
½ t. paprika
1 T. Worcestershire sauce
1 t. Kitchen Bouquet or low sodium browning sauce
1 T. low sodium ketchup
2 c. water

Add potatoes, carrots, onions, and frozen green beans to above. Simmer until cooked. Thicken with flour and water.

Per 1 ½ c. serving = 320 calories, 3 g saturated fat, 49 mg cholesterol, 125 mg sodium

GROUND BEEF AND VEGETABLE SOUP

Really low calorie. Soup fills the cavity!

1 lb. extra lean ground beef (or substitute ground turkey)
1 medium onion, chopped
½ tsp. minced garlic
4 c. Picante V8 Juice, low sodium variety
2 c. coleslaw mix
1 (15 oz) can no salt diced tomatoes
1 (10 oz) package frozen corn
1 (9 oz) package frozen green beans
2 T. Worcestershire sauce
1 t. basil
¼ t. pepper

Cook beef and onion; drain fat. Add remaining ingredients.
Cover and cook until heated through, or add remaining
ingredients to slow cooker and cook on high for 4 to 5 hours.

Per 1 c. serving = 169 calories, 1 g saturated fat, 30 mg cholesterol, 150 mg sodium

HERBED STEW WITH HEAT

My good friend Deb first made this stew for us when we were invited to their home for dinner a number of months after Jeff's heart attack. She knew Jeff was watching his sodium and saturated fat. This tasty stew doesn't have a speck of salt, but it has plenty of flavor. I reduced the heat a bit. Add mushrooms if you like.

2 lbs. round steak, cut into 1" cubes
2 T. canola oil
3 c. water
1 large onion, chopped
¾ t. pepper
1 t. rosemary
1 t. oregano
1 t. basil
¾ t. garlic powder
1 t. marjoram
2 bay leaves
1 (15 oz) can no salt diced tomatoes
1 (6 oz) can tomato paste
2 c. cubed peeled potatoes
2 c. sliced carrots
1 large green pepper, chopped
1 (9 oz) package frozen green beans
1 (10 oz) package frozen corn

Brown meat in oil in Dutch oven. Add water, diced tomatoes, tomato paste, onions and seasonings. Cover and simmer 1 ½ hours or until meat is tender. Stir in potatoes, carrots and green pepper. Simmer 30 minutes. Add more water if necessary. Stir in remaining ingredients and simmer additional 20 minutes.

Per 1 c. serving = 223 calories, 2 g saturated fat, 47 mg cholesterol, 83 mg sodium

MINESTRONE SOUP

Low sodium V8 juice and a host of beans and macaroni make this a zesty and filling soup. Use frozen Mediterranean Blend vegetables if you don't feel like chopping veggies. Borrowed from friends at Essentia Health.

2 T. basil olive oil
1 ½ c. onion, diced
1 ½ c. celery, diced
6 carrots, peeled and chopped
2 zucchini, chopped
1 (15 oz) can no salt diced tomatoes
1 (8 oz) can no salt tomato sauce
1 (5 oz) can low sodium V8 juice
½ c. red wine
2 t. oregano
½ t. garlic powder or 3 garlic cloves, chopped
½ t. pepper
2 t. basil
½ t. Tabasco Sauce
4 c. low sodium chicken or vegetable broth
1 (15 oz) can low sodium red kidney beans, drained and rinsed
1 (15 oz) can low sodium white beans, drained and rinsed
2 c. spinach
½ c. elbow macaroni

In Dutch oven, heat olive oil and sauté onions, garlic, celery and carrots (or use Mediterranean Blend vegetables instead) and sauté for 5 or 6 minutes. Add broth, tomatoes, and tomato sauce and V8 juice and bring to a boil. Add red wine. Reduce heat. Add remaining ingredients. Simmer 45 to 60 minutes.

Per 1 c. serving = 120 calories, 2.5 g fat, 0 saturated fat, 0 mg cholesterol, 150 mg sodium

PASTA PIZZA SOUP

A delicious soup on a cold Minnesota day. Another yummy recipe from the folks at Essentia Health.

1 lb. extra lean ground beef or turkey
1 medium onion, chopped
2 stalks celery, chopped
2 carrots, chopped
4 c. low sodium beef broth or water (if using water, add 1 T. low sodium beef bouillon)
1 (15 oz) can no salt diced tomatoes with basil, oregano and garlic
1 bay leaf
¼ t. garlic powder
1 ½ t. oregano
¼ t. Mrs. Dash tomato basil seasoning
1 ½ c. tricolor spiral pasta

In a large saucepan, cook beef or turkey, onion and celery until meat is no longer pink and vegetables are tender. Drain fat. Stir in beef broth, bay leaf and seasonings. Add 1 ½ c. tricolor spiral pasta. Bring to a boil. Reduce heat; cover and simmer until carrots and pasta are tender. Discard bay leaf.

Per 1 c. serving = 168 calories, 1 g saturated fat, 21 mg cholesterol, 153 mg sodium

RED LENTIL SOUP

I found this recipe in the Parade section of the Sunday newspaper. It has zip, and it is especially nutritious containing red lentils, barley and brown rice. I like to use the tomato paste in a tube, because you can use what you need and refrigerate the rest.

2 T. olive oil
2 c. diced carrots
1 c. diced onions
2 T. tomato paste
¾ t. roasted ground cumin
¾ c. red lentils
3 T. uncooked brown rice
½ c. barley
6 c. low sodium vegetable broth
¼ t. pepper

Heat oil in Dutch oven over medium heat. Add carrots and onion; cook, stirring occasionally until onion is softened, about 7 minutes. Add tomato paste and cumin; stir to combine. Add lentils, rice, barley, vegetable broth, and pepper. Bring to a boil. Reduce heat and simmer 30 minutes or until lentils, rice and barley are tender. Makes about 6 cups.

Per 1 c. serving = 246 calories, 7 g fat, less than 1 g saturated fat, 0 mg cholesterol, 107 mg sodium

TOMATO BASIL SOUP

This came from an Internet search and Taste of Home recipe. We enjoy the flavor of the tomatoes and basil blended together with a hint of carrot taste. We think this soup is extra delicious!

4 or 5 medium carrots, finely chopped
1 large yellow onion, chopped
1 large (49 oz) can reduced sodium chicken or vegetable broth (divided)
1 (29 oz) can no salt tomato puree
5 t. dried basil
1 ½ t. sugar (or Splenda)
½ t. pepper
1 (12 oz) can fat-free evaporated milk

In Dutch oven coated generously with cooking spray, cook carrots and onion over medium low heat for about 20 minutes until tender. Remove from heat and cool slightly.

In blender, place half the broth and cooled vegetables, cover and process until blended. Return to Dutch oven. Stir in tomato puree, basil, sugar, pepper and the remaining broth. Bring to a boil. Reduce heat; simmer uncovered 30 minutes. Reduce heat to low. Gradually stir in the evaporated milk; heat through (do not boil).

Per 1 c. serving = 115 calories, 0 fat, 0 cholesterol, 118 mg sodium

TURKEY BLACK BEAN CHILI

I found variations of this recipe in a low sodium cookbook and internet recipe search. I adjusted the seasonings a bit. It only has about 80 mg of sodium per serving. It tastes great anytime, but is especially good for dinner on cold Minnesota nights! And we have plenty of those!

1 ¼ lb. extra lean ground turkey
2 T. olive oil
1 yellow onion, chopped
1 green pepper, chopped
2 (15 oz each) cans low sodium black beans, rinsed and drained
1 (15 oz) can no salt diced tomatoes
1 (8 oz) can no salt tomato sauce
1 c. low sodium beef broth
1 (5 oz) can low sodium V8 juice
1 heaping T. chili powder
1 T. cumin
1 t. coriander
1 t. dried oregano
½ t. garlic powder

In Dutch oven over medium high heat, brown the meat in olive oil until no longer pink. Add onion and green pepper and cook until vegetables are tender, about 4 to 5 minutes. Add remaining ingredients. Bring to a boil, then reduce heat and simmer for 45 minutes until thickened, stirring occasionally. Add more beef broth if it is too thick.

Yield: 6 servings

Per 1 ½ c. serving = 350 calories, 2 g saturated fat, 58 mg cholesterol, 80 mg sodium

VEGETABLE BEEF SOUP

This recipe was adapted from one of those little recipe books that come with your slow cooker. I quit using peppercorns when our boys were young—they used to "find" the peppercorns and bite into them!

1 lb. appropriate beef (round steak, etc.), cubed
1 (15 oz) can no salt diced tomatoes
2 carrots, sliced
3 stalks celery with tops, sliced
3 medium potatoes, diced
2 medium onions, diced
3 c. water or low sodium beef broth
1 T. low sodium beef bouillon granules
¼ t. pepper (or 4 peppercorns!)
1 (9 oz) package frozen mixed vegetables

Brown beef; drain fat. Add remaining ingredients and simmer until vegetables are tender. Or, put all in a slow cooker and cook on high for 4 to 5 hours. If using slow cooker, add mixed vegetables during the last 2 hours of cooking.

Per 1 ½ c. serving = 380 calories, 2 g saturated fat, 80 mg cholesterol, 144 mg sodium

Toss Me A Salad

CAESAR DRESSING

Many Caesar dressings are very high in sodium. Making your own is best. Easy, too!

1/3 c. plain non-fat yogurt or fat-free mayonnaise
2 T. lemon juice
1 t. olive oil
1 t. white wine vinegar
1 t. Dijon mustard
1 t. Worcestershire sauce
¼ t. garlic powder or 1 clove garlic, crushed

Add dressing to romaine lettuce and cooked chicken breast. Add fat free croutons and ¼ c. grated parmesan cheese.

Per 2 T. serving = 188 calories, , 1.5 g saturated fat, 54 mg cholesterol, 328 mg sodium

CRANBERRY COLE SLAW

*This recipe came from a Penzey's Spice catalog a while ago.
Tweaked it a bit. It is especially festive during the holidays.
Replace the canola oil with a reduced fat olive oil mayonnaise
for a more traditional cole slaw.*

1 bag shredded cole slaw mix or cabbage
¼ c. red onion, sliced thin
1 ½ c. dried cranberries

Dressing:

1/3 c. apple cider vinegar
1/3 c. canola oil
2 t. red wine vinegar
1/3 c. sugar
1 t. celery seed

In large bowl, combine cole slaw mix/cabbage, onion and
cranberries; toss to combine. Whisk together dressing
ingredients. Pour over the slaw, cover and refrigerate overnight
or at least 3 hours. Drain off excess dressing before serving.

Per ¾ c. serving = 190 calories, 1 g saturated fat, 0 mg cholesterol, 15 mg sodium

EASY LOW FAT COLESLAW

Our tried and true coleslaw recipe. Adjust sugar and mustard to taste.

½ c. fat free mayonnaise or mayonnaise with olive oil
2 T. cider vinegar
Splash of red wine vinegar
1 t. Dijon mustard
2 t. sugar or Splenda
¼ t. celery seed
1 bag shredded coleslaw mix

Whisk ingredients. Empty coleslaw in large bowl. Pour dressing on top and toss. Thin with 1 to 2 T. low fat milk, if necessary.

Per ¾ c. serving = 48 calories, 0.8 g fat, 3 mg cholesterol, 194 mg sodium

FRUITY COLESLAW

A sweet coleslaw and a nice change from the usual and customary.

1 (16 oz) pkg. coleslaw mix
2 celery ribs, chopped
1 c. red seedless grapes, halved
1 medium Granny Smith apple, chopped
1 small carton plain yogurt (or lemon or orange flavored)
1/3 c. orange juice
2 T. fat free mayonnaise
1 T. sugar (or Splenda)
1 T. lemon juice

Combine coleslaw mix, celery, grapes and apple in large bowl. Combine remaining ingredients, pour over top. Toss to coat. Cover and refrigerator for at least 2 hours prior to serving.

Per ¾ c. serving = 50 calories, trace saturated fat, 1 mg cholesterol, 51 mg sodium

LUSH LETTUCE SALAD

A recipe from my Aunt Bev. A bit changed from the original, but just as tasty! This one always gets rave reviews whenever it is served.

1 bag of lettuce – we prefer Romaine
3 green onions, chopped
1 c. low sodium chow mein noodles
3 T. sesame seeds
6 oz. unsalted, chopped cashews
4 strips of center cut bacon, fried crisp, chopped
Dressing:
4 T. sugar, ½ t. pepper, ½ t. Mrs. Dash Original Blend seasoning, ¼ t. celery seed, ½ c. canola oil, 2 T. apple cider vinegar.

Place lettuce and onions in large bowl. Just before serving, add chow mein noodles, sesame seeds, cashews and bacon.

Mix salad dressing ingredients together and mix well. Pour over salad.

Yield: 8 servings

Per ¾ c. serving = 184 calories, 0 saturated fat, 85 mg sodium

SAVORY POTATO SALAD

Vegetables give the crunch and spicy mustard provides the savory flavor in this delicious potato salad.

6 medium red potatoes
2 stalks celery, finely chopped
2 green onions, finely chopped
¼ c. red pepper, chopped
¼ c. green pepper, chopped
1 T. yellow onion, finely chopped
2 hard-boiled eggs, chopped
½ cucumber, chopped, optional
Radishes, sliced, optional
6 T. light mayonnaise
1 t. spicy brown mustard
1/8 t. salt
¼ t. pepper
¼ t. dill weed

Wash potatoes, cut each in half, and place in pan in cold water. Cook covered over medium heat 25 to 30 minutes or until just tender. Drain; dice potatoes when cool. Add vegetables and eggs to potatoes and toss. Blend mayonnaise and spices. Pour over potatoes and stir gently. Chill at least one hour before serving.

Per ¾ c. serving = 98 calories, 2 g fat, 0.5 g saturated fat, 21 mg cholesterol, 185 mg sodium

SPINACH SALAD WITH ORANGES

Sometimes you just need something sweet and salty. Mandarin oranges give the sweet and bacon provides the salty in this dish. And spinach is added for good nutrition!

1 (10 oz) pkg. fresh spinach
1 (11 oz) can no sugar added mandarin oranges, drain juice
3 or 4 bacon strips, center cut, cooked and crumbled
1 c. sliced fresh mushrooms, optional
Dressing:
3 T. low sodium ketchup
2 T. cider vinegar
1 ½ t. Worcestershire sauce
¼ c. sugar
2 T. finely chopped onion
1/8 t. salt
1/8 t. pepper
½ c. canola oil

In large bowl, toss the spinach, oranges and bacon; set aside. Combine remaining ingredients and mix until smooth (or use a blender to process until smooth).

Per 1 c. serving = 206 calories, 1.7 g saturated fat, 2.5 mg cholesterol, 95 mg sodium

STRAWBERRY SPINACH SALAD I

Mom and I went strawberry picking for many years. This recipe came from Finke's Berry Farm, and we served it often.

½ pint (or more) strawberries, sliced
1 bag of spinach (or romaine lettuce, or spinach/romaine blend)
Dressing:
¼ c. canola oil
2 T. apple cider vinegar
¼ c. sugar (or Splenda)
1/8 t. paprika
1/8 t. Worcestershire sauce
½ t. poppy seed
1 t. sesame seed
1/3 c. unsalted, sliced almonds (optional)

Combine dressing, drizzle over salad, and toss.

Per 1 c. serving = 142 calories, 1 g saturated fat, 0 cholesterol, 40 mg sodium

STRAWBERRY SALAD II

Always looking for another good strawberry salad recipe. This one fit the bill. Can't remember where it came from.

Real bacon bits – lowest sodium available, or 3 strips center cut bacon, fry crisp, use paper towel to absorb grease when bacon is done.
3 T. rice vinegar
2 T. honey
5 t. olive oil
1 t. Dijon type mustard
½ t. pepper
1/8 t. celery seed
1 (6 oz) bag baby spinach
2 medium oranges, peeled or chopped, or 1 can mandarin oranges, drained
½ pint (or more) strawberries, quartered
1 cucumber, thinly sliced
1 medium carrot, shredded
Optional: ½ c. chopped walnuts

In a small bowl, whisk vinegar, honey, oil, mustard and pepper and celery seed.

In another bowl, combine spinach, oranges, strawberries, cucumber and carrot. Pour dressing over salad; toss to coat. Sprinkle with bacon bits, and walnuts, if desired.

Per 1 c. serving = 126 calories, 94 mg sodium, 1 g saturated fat, 3 mg cholesterol, 148 mg sodium

Make It A Savory Side

BAKED BASIL WEDGES

Everyone who tries these remarks on the great flavor! We always make a big batch, because most everyone has seconds! Thanks to Essential Cardiac Rehab Center for this one.

½ c. Parmesan cheese
2 T. basil olive oil
2 T. dried basil
½ t. garlic powder
10 baby red potatoes

In a large bowl, combine Parmesan cheese, oil, and basil and garlic powder. Cut potatoes into wedges or fries. Add to cheese mixture; toss to coat. Place in a large jelly roll pan coated with nonstick cooking spray. Bake at 425 degrees for 15 minutes, Turn potatoes and bake 8 minutes additional or until crisp and tender.

Yield: 8 servings

Per serving = 162 calories, 5 g fat, 5 mg cholesterol, 117 mg sodium

COMPANY MASHED TATERS

I had two different "company potato" recipes that I blended together for this one; Aunt Bev had one and Judy used a variation. This one can be prepared ahead of time and refrigerated until ready to place in the oven.

11 (or so) large potatoes, cooked and mashed (add low fat milk, margarine/butter, etc.)
Add: 1 (8 oz) carton fat free sour cream
1 (8 oz) fat free cream cheese
3 t. chopped chives
½ t. pepper
½ c. low fat shredded cheddar cheese
Parsley and paprika for garnish

Mix all ingredients. Place prepared potatoes in a 9x13 casserole dish (sprayed with non-stick cooking spray). Sprinkle with parsley flakes and paprika. Cover and bake, 350 degree oven until hot (45 minutes).

Yield: 8 to 10 servings

Per serving = 209 calories, 2 g fat, 8 mg cholesterol, 187 mg sodium

CROCKPOT BEANS

There is way too much sodium in canned baked beans. These are a decent alternative.

4 (15 oz each) cans low sodium beans (kidney, black, or your choice)
¼ c. brown sugar
¼ c. molasses
1 large onion, chopped
1 c. water
1 T. balsamic vinegar
1 T. low sodium barbeque sauce
2 T. low sodium ketchup
1/8 t. cayenne pepper
¼ t. garlic powder
¼ t. dry mustard
2 T. cornstarch mixed with 2 T. water

Add all to crock pot. Cook on high for 4 hours, or on low for 6 to 8 hours.

Per ¾ c. serving = 129 calories, 1 g fat, 118 mg sodium

GARLIC-DILL SMASHED POTATOES

Take 3 cloves of garlic, wrap in heavy duty aluminum foil and drizzle with ½ t. olive oil: Bake them or grill them.

1 lb. red potatoes, washed and halved
2 T. low fat milk
2 T. fat free sour cream
2 t. Parmesan cheese
1 t. fresh dill or ½ t. dill weed
1/8 t. pepper
Dash of Tabasco sauce

Bake aluminum foiled wrapped garlic in 425 degree oven for 15 minutes and cool for 10 minutes. Place potatoes in saucepan and cover with water. Bring to boil, reduce heat and cook until tender about 20 minutes. Drain. Transfer potatoes to bowl and squeeze softened garlic into bowl. Add remaining ingredients and mash. Serve immediately.

Yield: 4 to 6 servings

Per serving = 165 calories, 2 g fat, 1 g saturated fat, 6 mg cholesterol, 159 mg sodium

PARSLEY SMASHED POTATOES

Fresh parsley and chives from the garden and the red skins of the potatoes makes a colorful side dish. These are nice and creamy.

2 lbs. baby red potatoes
2/3 c. plain yogurt
2 T. snipped fresh chives
¼ c. chopped fresh parsley
2 T. light butter
¼ t. pepper

Boil potatoes until tender; mash. Combine other ingredients in large bowl. Mix cooked potatoes into yogurt mix. Serve immediately.

Yield: 6 to 8 servings

Per ¾ c. serving = 52 calories, 2 g saturated fat; 12 mg cholesterol, 47 mg sodium

ROASTED VEGETABLES

Vegetables from the garden or local Famers' Market, or your favorite fresh or frozen vegetables roasted in the oven or placed on the grill in aluminum foil are so delicious!

Toss 6 to 8 cups of your favorite fresh or frozen vegetable combinations, cut into bite sized pieces with ¼ c. extra virgin olive oil (we especially like basil or Tuscan herb olive oil). Season with ¼ t. salt (or Mrs. Dash original seasoning blend) and ¼ t. black pepper, or your favorite no-salt blend, and spread evenly in a baking pan.

Bake at 425 degrees for 20 to 30 minutes.

If placing on a grill, put the vegetables in a grill pan or in aluminum foil and cook over medium heat.

Good roasted vegetable combinations include Mediterranean Blend or Zucchini, Carrots, Peppers and Onions. Your choice.

Yield: 8 to 10 servings

Per ¾ c. serving = Approximately 80 calories, depending on veggie type, 1 or 2 g saturated fat, 50 to 70 mg sodium

ROASTED ZUCCHINI

You can't go wrong with roasted vegetables, especially plentiful zucchini!

2 medium zucchini
1 T. basil olive oil
1 t. dried oregano
¼ c. Parmesan cheese
1/8 t. pepper

Slice zucchini. Toss with oil and oregano. Arrange on baking sheet sprayed with nonstick olive oil spray. Sprinkle with Parmesan cheese and pepper. Bake at 350 degrees for 20 minutes or until tender.

Yield: 6 servings

Per ¾ c. serving = 67 calories, 5 g fat, 1 g saturated fat, 4 mg cholesterol, 96 mg sodium

SCALLOPED CORN

A good alternative to the canned cream corn style baked corn typically consumed at Thanksgiving. And I can never find low sodium canned cream corn anyway.

¼ c. chopped onion
2 T. light tub margarine
2 T. flour
¼ t. salt
½ t. paprika
¼ t. dry mustard
1/ 8 t. pepper
¾ c. low fat milk
1 (10 oz) pkg. frozen corn
1 egg
Low sodium crackers, green pepper, pimientos for garnish

Preheat oven to 350 degrees. Sauté onion in margarine until golden. Blend in flour, seasonings; cook until bubbly. Remove from heat. Gradually add milk. Bring to boil; boil 1 minute, stirring constantly. Remove from heat. Add corn and egg. Pour into one qt. baking dish sprayed with nonstick spray. Top with low sodium cracker crumbs, green pepper and pimientos.

Yield: 4 to 6 servings

Per serving = 143 calories, 4 g fat, 0 mg cholesterol. 178 mg sodium

SIMPLE SCALLOPED POTATOES (MICROWAVE)

I enjoy having Au gratin and scalloped potatoes, especially during holiday times. I found this recipe years and years ago, and it is a pretty tasty alternative to the "cream of mushroom/ cheddar cheese soup" type. Double the recipe and use a large covered casserole dish that fits in your microwave. Can also be prepared in a convection oven.

5 c. (approximately 4 large peeled and sliced) potatoes
1 T. flour
¼ c. chopped onion or 1 T. instant minced onion
1 ½ c. low fat milk
1 T. light tub margarine
Paprika or parsley for garnish (optional)

In 2 ½ or 3 qt. (microwave safe) casserole coated with nonstick spray, arrange sliced potatoes. Add flour and onion; toss lightly. Stir in milk and dot with margarine. Cook, covered tightly in microwave, 15 minutes or until potatoes are desired doneness, stirring 3 or 4 times. If desired, sprinkle with paprika or parsley. Let stand, covered, 3 minutes to finish cooking.

Yield: 4 to 6 servings

Per serving = 189 calories, 2 g fat, 11 mg cholesterol, 78 mg sodium

SWISS SCALLOPED POTATOES

These traditional down-home potatoes are so good that even the calorie-conscious, low sodium counters will think they are cheating! This adapted recipe came from Taste of Home Cooking.

2 ½ lbs. sliced peeled potatoes
4 c. fat free or low fat milk
½ t. garlic powder
¼ t. rosemary
¼ t. white pepper
1 bay leaf
4 t. cornstarch
2 T. cold water
4 oz. reduced fat shredded Swiss cheese
1 ½ c. low sodium bread crumbs
2 T. low sodium tub margarine

In Dutch oven, combine potatoes, milk, garlic, pepper, rosemary and bay leaf. Bring to a boil. Reduce heat to low; cover and cook for 8 minutes or until almost tender. Discard bay leaf.

In small bowl combine cornstarch and cold water until smooth; stir into potato mixture. Bring to a boil. Reduce heat and stir for 2 minutes. Remove from heat; stir in cheese.

Transfer to 9x13 baking dish coated with nonstick spray. Combine bread crumbs and butter; sprinkle over potatoes. Bake uncovered at 350 degrees for 30 minutes or until bubbly and crumbs are golden brown.

Yield: 12 servings

Per serving = 190 calories, 6 g fat, 3.5 g saturated fat, 17 mg cholesterol, 85 mg sodium

THREE GRAIN PILAF

This is a tasty side dish when you are looking for something a little different than ordinary.

1 large onion, chopped
2/3 c. shredded carrot
2 T. olive oil (or basil olive oil)
1/3 c. uncooked brown rice
1/3 c. uncooked barley
1/3 c. uncooked bulger
2 c. low sodium vegetable or chicken broth
¼ c. red wine or water
¼ t. dried oregano
¼ t. garlic powder
¼ t. basil
¼ t. pepper
1 T. dried parsley
1/3 t. sliced almonds, toasted

In large nonstick skillet, sauté onion and carrots until crisp-tender, about 3 minutes. Stir in the rice, barley and bulger; sauté until grains are lightly browned or about 4 minutes. Gradually add broth and wine or water. Bring to a boil. Reduce heat; stir in seasonings. Cover and simmer for 40 minutes or until grains are tender and liquid is absorbed. Sprinkle with almonds.

Yield: 4 or 5 servings

Per serving = 238 calories, 9 g fat, 1 g saturated fat, 0 cholesterol, 84 mg sodium

TWICE BAKED POTATOES

Most everyone loves twice baked potatoes! Switch up the spices to change the flavor to complement your meal.

4 medium russet potatoes
¾ c. cottage cheese
¼ c. low fat milk
2 T. low fat tub margarine
1 t. dill weed
¾ t. Mrs. Dash Original Blend seasoning
2 drops Tabasco sauce
¼ c. Parmesan cheese

Prick potatoes with fork. Bake at 425 degrees for 60 minutes or until fork is easily inserted. Cut potatoes in half lengthwise. Carefully scoop out potato leaving about ½ inch of pulp inside shell. Mash pulp in large bowl. Mix remaining ingredients except Parmesan cheese, and spoon mixture into potato shells. Sprinkle top of each potato with Parmesan cheese. Place on baking sheet and return to oven. Bake 15 to 20 minutes until golden brown.

A variation of twice baked potatoes: Omit cottage cheese. Mix potato pulp, milk and margarine. Spoon into potato shells. Sprinkle with shredded Swiss cheese and paprika. Bake as above.

Yield: 8 servings

Per ½ potato serving = 113 calories, 4 g fat, 1.5 g saturated fat, 40 mg cholesterol, 150 mg sodium

Gather Around the Dinner Table

ALMOST GIADA'S TURKEY MEATBALLS

Jeff is a big Giada fan. This one came to be while watching a cooking show featuring Giada. The basic ingredients are based on Giada's, but it's lightened up a bit. It's pretty tasty, especially with the tomato sauce recipe (adapted) that follows.

1 lb. extra lean turkey
1 small onion, finely chopped
3 cloves garlic, minced (or ½ t. garlic powder)
1 egg
¼ to ½ c. low sodium bread crumbs (or use oatmeal)
3 T. low sodium ketchup
¼ c. fresh parsley (or use chopped spinach)
¼ c. Parmesan cheese
¼ c. Romano cheese
1/8 t. salt
¼ t. pepper

In a large bowl combine onion, garlic, egg, bread crumbs, ketchup, parsley (or spinach), Parmesan and Romano cheese, salt and pepper. Mix in turkey. Roll into small meatballs.

Bake at 400 degrees for 9 minutes; turn over and bake additional 9 minutes. Broil for 2 minutes if meatballs need to brown.

Yield: About 40 meatballs.

Per serving (2 meatballs) = 48 calories, 1 g saturated fat, 15 mg cholesterol, 68 mg sodium

COOKING SHOW TOMATO SAUCE

Basic ingredients in this one are again based on Giada's recipe, modified to our taste. This recipe makes a lot, so freeze sauce for up to 6 months in 2 c. portions.

½ c. extra virgin olive oil
1 small onion, chopped
2 cloves garlic, chopped
1 stalk celery, chopped
1 carrot, chopped
Pepper to taste
2 (32 oz) cans crushed tomatoes (no salt)
4 to 6 basil leaves (or 1 ½ T. dried basil)
2 bay leaves
1 t. Italian seasoning
1 t. dried oregano

Heat oil over medium high heat. Sauté onion and garlic about 2 minutes. Add celery and carrot, season with pepper. Sauté until soft, about 5 minutes. Add tomatoes, basil, bay leaves and seasonings. Add half the sauce to food processor, then other half. Process until smooth. Place desired amount of sauce into Dutch oven or slow cooker; heat through.

Per ¼ c. serving = 40 calories, 0 saturated fat, 25 mg sodium

AMISH ROAST

We found this recipe in a Penzey's Spice catalog. The roast cooks for 5 (yes, 5) hours, but it is moist, tender, and well worth the wait. We have also used pork roast, and it is equally delicious. Hint: Use latex kitchen gloves when putting the "paste" on the roast.

2 ½ to 3 lb. beef roast (round or sirloin)
1 lb. carrots, peeled and cut into thirds
1 large onion, peeled and quartered
6 to 8 potatoes, peeled and quartered
2 T. spicy brown mustard
1 T. Worcestershire sauce
1 t. marjoram
1 t. allspice
¼ t. black pepper
1 c. water

Preheat oven to 350 degrees. Rinse roast and pat dry. In large roasting pan or Dutch oven, combine vegetables. In small bowl, combine mustard, Worcestershire sauce, marjoram and allspice to make a paste. Rub the paste all over the roast and place the roast on top of the vegetables. Sprinkle with pepper. Pour water in the bottom of the pan. Cover and cook at 350 degrees for 1 hour. Reduce heat to 200 degrees and cook for another 3 to 4 hours. Let rest 10 minutes before slicing.

Yield: 8 servings

Per 2 slices of roast and 1 cup of vegetables = 310 calories, 6 g fat, 75 mg cholesterol, 380 mg sodium

AMORE ITALIAN CHICKEN

We especially enjoy Italian food. This recipe originally called for making it on the stove top. I prefer it baked in the oven.

1 medium onion, chopped
1 1/8 t. paprika, divided
2 t. basil olive oil
1 ¼ c. water
¼ c. tomato paste
1 bay leaf
½ t. low sodium chicken bouillon
½ t. Italian seasoning, no salt
¼ c. flour
1 ½ t. Parmesan cheese
¼ t. garlic powder
¼ t. oregano
¼ t. Mrs. Dash Original Blend or Tomato Basil seasoning
1 ½ lbs. chicken (tenderloins or breasts)

Sauté onion and 1/8 t. paprika in basil olive oil until tender. Stir in water, tomato paste, bay leaf, bouillon, and Italian seasoning. Bring to a boil. Reduce heat and simmer, uncovered for 10 minutes. Set aside.

In a large resealable plastic bag, combine flour, Parmesan cheese, garlic powder, oregano, Mrs. Dash seasoning and remaining paprika. Add chicken; seal bag and shake to coat.

Place coated chicken in bottom of 9x13 baking pan sprayed with nonstick spray. Pour tomato mixture over top. Discard bay leaf. Bake at 375 degrees for 45 minutes or until juices run clear.

Yield: 6 servings

Per serving = 168 calories, trace saturated fat, 67 mg cholesterol, 154 mg sodium

AUNT ELAINE'S PEPPER STEAK

My godmother's recipe with a few adjustments to reduce sodium.

1 lb. round steak
¼ c. canola oil
½ t. Mrs. Dash Original Blend seasoning
¼ t. garlic powder
Dash pepper
¼ c. diced onion
4 green peppers cut into 1 inch pieces
1 c. celery
1 c. low sodium beef broth
2 T. cornstarch
¼ c. cold water
2 t. soy sauce substitute (see recipe on page 41)

Cut steak diagonally into thin slices, about 2 inches. Preheat electric skillet at 375 degrees. Brown meat. Add oil, Mrs. Dash seasoning, garlic powder and pepper. Set control at 210 degrees. Add onions, green pepper, celery and beef broth. Cover and cook until crisply tender – about 10 minutes. (Add hot water, if necessary). Blend cornstarch, cold water and soy sauce substitute. Add to meat mixture and cook and stir until thickened, about 5 minutes.

Yield: 4 large servings

Per serving = 279 calories, 3.5 g saturated fat, 101 mg sodium

BAKED ORANGE CHICKEN

I adapted this recipe from a Taste of Home recipe. Soy sauce in the original recipe made the sodium levels high, so use the substitute below (also found in the condiment section, page 41).

1 c. orange juice
2 T. soy sauce substitute (see recipe following—use 2 T., refrigerate remaining for another use)
4 boneless chicken breasts
4 T. or more orange marmalade

Make soy sauce substitute: 2 T. sodium free beef bouillon, 2 t. red wine vinegar, 1 t. molasses, 1/8 t. ginger, dash black pepper, dash garlic powder, ¾ c. water. Combine all ingredients; boil gently uncovered 5 minutes or until mixture reduced to ½ c. Stir before using.

In small bowl, combine orange juice and soy sauce substitute. Pour ½ c. marinade into large reseal able bag; add chicken. Seal bag and turn to coat. Refrigerate for at least one hour; longer if possible. Cover and refrigerate remaining marinade.

Drain and discard marinade from bag. Place chicken and reserved marinade in baking dish coated with cooking spray. Spoon marmalade over chicken.

Bake uncovered at 350 degrees for 40 to 45 minutes or until chicken juices run clear. Top chicken with additional marmalade about 5 to 7 minutes before done.

Yield: 4 servings

Per serving: 187 calories, 3 g fat, 1 g saturated fat, 63 mg cholesterol, 117 mg sodium

BETTY'S SUKIYAKI

My mom made a decent sukiyaki that she based on an old Betty Crocker recipe. I modified the recipe by making it more heart healthy, losing the high sodium soy sauce and replacing it with soy sauce substitute (found in the condiment section, page 41). Beef broth is now made with low sodium bouillon, broth base, or stock. Quick to make and easy clean up. A keeper.

1 lb. sirloin steak
2 T. canola oil
1 c. low sodium beef broth or stock
2 T. sugar
1/3 c. soy sauce substitute (see page 41))
2 large onions, thinly sliced
3 stalks celery, diagonally sliced
1 (8 oz) can bamboo shoots, rinsed and drained
1 (8 oz) can water chestnuts, rinsed and drained
(Also add mushrooms and spinach, if desired).

Cut sirloin across the grain into 2 inch long strips. In electric skillet, brown meat in oil. Push meat to one section of skillet. Stir in beef broth, sugar and soy sauce substitute.

Place onions, celery, bamboo shoots, water chestnuts (and mushrooms if desired) in separate sections of skillet. Do not mix. Cover; simmer 10 minutes. Add spinach if desired and simmer 5 minutes longer. Serve over brown rice.

Yield: 4 servings

Per serving = 270 calories, 2.5 g saturated fat, 110 mg sodium

CHICKEN CAPRESE

Found this recipe when checking out the Mrs. Dash website. With flattened chicken breasts, this one doesn't take long to make, but is a bit putzy in the roll up department. Fancy enough to make for company.

2 T. Mrs. Dash Tomato Basil seasoning
4 boneless, skinless chicken breasts, flattened to ¼" thickness
8 grape or cherry tomatoes, cut in quarters
4 low fat mozzarella string cheese sticks, cut in small pieces
1 T. basil olive oil
2 t. red wine vinegar

Toss tomatoes with 1 T. Mrs. Dash seasoning. Place tomatoes and mozzarella on each chicken breast. Roll up; secure with toothpicks. Place breasts on baking tray. Drizzle with olive oil, vinegar and remaining 1 T. Mrs. Dash seasoning.

Bake at 350 degrees for 35 to 40 minutes or until juices run clear. Remove from oven; cover lightly with foil. Let rest for 5 to 10 minutes before serving.

Yield: 4 servings

Per serving = 248 calories, 2 gm fat, 10 mg cholesterol, 74 mg sodium

CHICKEN MANICOTTI

This recipe is a family favorite. Make Italian sausage ahead of time. Use some for manicotti, some for cauliflower crust pizza later, and freeze the rest for another use. Manicotti is put together easily, as uncooked chicken is stuffed into uncooked manicotti shells, and store bought spaghetti sauce (low sodium, of course) is used. I have had many requests for this recipe. It's a keeper for sure!

2 t. garlic powder (or to taste)
1 t. Italian seasoning
1 ½ lbs. boneless skinless chicken breasts
16 uncooked manicotti shells
2 jars (26 oz. each) low sodium spaghetti sauce, divided
1 lb. Italian sausage, cooked and drained (see Italian sausage recipe, page 113)
4 c. reduced fat shredded mozzarella cheese (2 c. per pan)
¼ to 1/3 c. water

Rub garlic powder and Italian seasoning over chicken. Cut chicken into approximately 1" strips. Spread 2/3 c. spaghetti sauce in the bottom of two 9x13 pans that have been coated with nonstick spray. Place 8 stuffed manicotti shells in each dish. Sprinkle with sausage. Pour remaining spaghetti sauce over the top. Sprinkle with cheese. Add approximately ¼ to 1/3 c. water around the edge of each dish. (I take the spaghetti sauce jar, add a small amount of water, and drizzle the water around the edge of each dish).

Cover and bake at 375 degrees for 65 to 70 minutes or until chicken juices run clear and pasta is tender.

If you don't bake both pans, cover and freeze remaining casserole for up to one month. To use the frozen dish, thaw in the refrigerator, then let stand at room temperature for 20 minutes. Then bake as above.

Yield: 8 servings (2 pans)

Per serving (2 shells) = 385 calories, 3 g saturated fat, 100 mg cholesterol, 330 mg sodium

CHICKEN RICE AND BROCCOLI BAKE

My mom used to make a recipe called "Peekaboo Chicken." It was a one-dish chicken and rice casserole. It was good, but it had way too much sodium, as it used onion soup mix and cream of mushroom soup. I put together this recipe instead. It is similar...or close enough....with minimal sodium.

1 ½ c. long cooking rice
1 recipe condensed cream of broccoli soup (see below)
1 ½ c. low sodium chicken broth or stock
1 ½ c. water or stock
Rest of bag of frozen broccoli
6 chicken pieces
Paprika and parsley

To make condensed cream of broccoli soup: ½ c. frozen broccoli, ½ c. chopped onion, ½ c. low sodium chicken broth, 1 T. parsley, ¼ t. garlic powder, 2/3 c. non-dairy creamer, 2 T. cornstarch

To make soup: Cook broccoli, onion and spices until soft. Process in blender or food processer until well pureed. Shake together creamer and cornstarch until dissolved. Cook and stir until thick. Stir in vegetable mixture.

Mix together rice, soup, broth and water in the bottom of a 9x13 baking pan, coated with nonstick spray. Stir in remaining broccoli. Top with chicken pieces. Sprinkle paprika and parsley on top.   Bake at 375 degrees about 1 hour or until chicken is done and rice is tender.

Yield: 6 servings

Per serving = 161 calories, 2 g fat, 1 g saturated fat, 35 mg cholesterol, 134 mg sodium

CHICKEN WITH COCOA TOMATO SAUCE

Jeff and I were watching the Food Network and came across this one. Paula Deen was making a similar dish. We tried to remember ingredients and experimented a bit. The basic ingredients are based on Paula Deen's recipe but I slimmed it down and changed a few seasonings to our taste. The cocoa provides great flavor. Really!

4 chicken breasts or 6 chicken thighs (we prefer thighs)
¼ t. black pepper
Basil olive oil for cooking (about 3 T.)
1 large onion, chopped
2 cloves minced garlic
2 c. no salt tomato sauce
2 c. no salt diced tomatoes with basil, oregano and garlic
½ c. chicken stock or broth
1 T. cocoa powder
1 t. oregano
1 t. basil
1 t. sugar
2 t. parsley
1 t. Italian seasoning

Season chicken with pepper. Heat 2 T. basil olive oil over medium heat. Add chicken and cook until browned, about 10 minutes each side. Remove chicken; set aside. Add remaining 1 T. basil olive oil, onion and garlic and cook 2 minutes, stirring often. Add tomato sauce, diced tomatoes, chicken broth, cocoa, oregano, basil, sugar, parsley, and Italian seasoning. Stir until blended. Return chicken to pan, cover and simmer 15 minutes. Turn chicken over and continue cooking, covered for 15 minutes or until done. Serve over your favorite pasta.

Per serving (1 piece of chicken and ½ c. sauce) = 235 calories, 1.5 g saturated fat, 70 mg cholesterol, 205 mg sodium

CHICKEN/TURKEY A LA KING

This recipe came about after Thanksgiving a couple of years ago. It doesn't have the fattening white sauce, instead using fat free evaporated milk. Good use of leftover turkey.

1 t. light tub margarine
¼ c. green pepper, chopped
2 c. low sodium chicken broth or stock
1 (5 oz) can fat free evaporated milk
¼ t. salt
¼ t. pepper
¼ t. savory
1/3 c. flour
1/3 c. water
2. c. diced chicken or turkey
Small jar of pimentos
2 T. red wine or red wine vinegar
3 drops hot pepper sauce or ¼ t. red pepper flakes
1 T. parsley for garnish

Sauté green pepper in margarine. Whisk in broth, milk, salt, pepper and savory. In small bowl, whisk flour and water. Whisk into green pepper mixture. Bring to boil over medium high heat, stirring occasionally. Reduce heat to medium low and cook 2 to 3 minutes until thickened. Stir in chicken or turkey and pimentos. Heat thoroughly. Stir in red wine or red wine vinegar and hot pepper sauce or red pepper flakes. Spoon over toast or rice and sprinkle with parsley.

Per ¾ c. serving = 267 calories, 3 g fat, 1 g saturated fat, 36 mg cholesterol, 331 mg sodium

CHILI TORTILLA BAKE

This is our "go to" Mexican recipe. I make it quite often. Black beans and whole wheat or whole grain tortillas are ingredients in this dish. The whole grain tortillas have more sodium than corn, so sometimes I swap for corn tortillas. Delicious either way.

1 lb. extra lean ground beef (or use ground turkey)
1 (8 oz) can no salt tomato sauce
1 (15 oz) can no salt diced tomatoes
1 (5 oz) can vegetable juice (low sodium V8)
1 (15 oz) can low sodium black beans, rinsed and drained
1 c. frozen corn
1 (4 oz) can green chilies
2 T. (dried) minced onion
2 T. chili powder
1 t. cumin
½ t. garlic powder
½ t. oregano
4 oz. reduced fat shredded cheddar cheese
6 whole wheat or whole grain tortillas

In large skillet, cook beef over medium heat until no longer pink; drain fat. Stir in tomato sauce, beans, corn, green chilies, onion and spices; heat through.

In 9x13 baking dish coated with cooking spray layer half of the tortillas, beef or turkey mixture and shredded cheese. Repeat layers. Bake uncovered 35 to 40 minutes or until bubbly.

Yield: 6 servings

With 95% lean ground beef and reduced fat cheddar = 413 calories, 4 g saturated fat, 56 mg cholesterol, 173 mg sodium

CINDY'S MEAT LOAF

We don't eat red meat often, but every once in a while, we crave a meat loaf. Even with extra lean ground beef, it is a bit higher in saturated fat. But by using extra lean ground turkey, it's a pretty decent lower fat version of meat loaf.

1 ½ lbs. extra lean ground beef (or ground turkey)
1 c. oatmeal
1 onion, finely chopped
1 T. Penzey's red and green bell pepper (or ¼ c. diced green pepper)
1 egg
¼ t. black pepper
1 (8 oz) can no salt tomato sauce
½ c. water
2 t. Worcestershire sauce
3 T. cider vinegar
2 T. spicy brown mustard
3 T. brown sugar

Mix together meat, oatmeal, onion, Penzey's bell pepper, egg and black pepper and half the tomato sauce. Form into 1 large loaf or 2 small ones. Mix remaining ingredients together and pour over loaves. Bake at 350 degrees for 1 ½ hours.

Yield: 6 servings

Per serving with extra lean ground beef = 389 calories, 3.5 g saturated fat, 113 mg cholesterol, 116 mg sodium

CRANBERRY CHICKEN

This recipe was borrowed from the folks at Essentia Health's Cardiac Rehab Center and adapted from Taste of Home Low Fat Country Cooking. It's a good top-of-the-stove recipe.

½ c. flour
¼ t. pepper
6 boneless skinless chicken breasts
3 T. canola oil
1 c. water or low sodium chicken stock or broth
1 c. fresh or frozen cranberries
½ c. brown sugar
1/8 t. nutmeg
1/8 t. allspice
1 T. red wine vinegar

In shallow dish, combine flour and pepper; dredge chicken. In skillet, heat canola oil over medium heat. Brown chicken on both sides. Remove and keep warm. In same skillet, combine water, cranberries, brown sugar, nutmeg, allspice and vinegar. Cook and stir until the berries burst, about 5 minutes. Return chicken to skillet. Cover and simmer for 30 minutes or until chicken is tender, basting occasionally with the sauce.

Yield: 6 servings

Per serving = 284 calories, 9 g fat, 1 g saturated fat, 73 mg cholesterol, 122 mg sodium

CROCKPOT CHICKEN CACCIATORE

This recipe came from a low sodium website. We felt the original recipe needed more sauce, so modified it accordingly.

1 large onion, sliced
6 boneless chicken breasts
2 (6 oz) cans tomato paste
1 (8 oz) can no salt tomato sauce
¼ t. black pepper
½ t. garlic powder
1 t. oregano
1 t. basil
½ t. Italian seasoning
¼ c. dry white wine
¼ c. water

Place onion in bottom of slow cooker. Place chicken on top of onions. Combine the rest of the ingredients and pour over chicken. Cook on low 8 to 10 hours.

Yield: 6 servings

Per serving = 112 calories, 2 g fat, 0 saturated fat, 34 mg cholesterol, 87 mg sodium

FAMILY GOULASH

This is also known as "Gunderson Goulash" at our house, as our friends were the ones who introduced us to this recipe quite a few years ago. Now, of course, it has been adapted to be low sodium. With a green salad and low sodium bread or rolls, it makes a hearty dinner.

½ pkg. (8 oz) egg noodles
1 lb. extra lean ground beef or ground turkey
1 medium onion, chopped
2 c. celery, chopped
½ c. low sodium ketchup
1 (15 oz) can no salt tomatoes
1 t. Mrs. Dash Tomato Basil seasoning
¼ t. pepper

Cook egg noodles, drain, and set aside. Cook ground beef or ground turkey and onion in large skillet until meat is no longer pink and onion is tender. Drain fat. In same skillet, stir in noodles, celery, ketchup, tomatoes, Mrs. Dash seasoning and pepper. Cover and simmer 40 minutes.

Yield: 4 servings

Per serving = 282 calories, 2 g fat, 45 mg cholesterol, 212 mg sodium

ITALIAN SAUSAGE

We use this recipe for a host of things including pizza, manicotti, spaghetti, burgers. Make 3 lbs. and use some for dinner, refrigerate some for your next day's meal, and freeze the remaining to use later. Courtesy of Essentia Health Cardiac Rehab Center.

3 lbs. ground pork sirloin or very lean ground pork
5 t. oregano
3 ½ t. basil
3 ½ t. garlic powder
2 t. parsley
2 t. sugar
1 ½ t. red pepper
1 t. fennel seed
1. t. anise seed

Mix ingredients and refrigerate overnight so flavors can blend. Brown sausage. Freeze unused (browned) portions.

Per 4 oz. serving = 175 calories, 7 g fat, 2.5 g saturated fat, 70 mg cholesterol, 60 mg sodium

MAJOR LEAGUE MANICOTTI

After the Twins won the World Series in 1991, I found myself the owner of a Minnesota Twins cookbook. I made a number of the recipes, including a manicotti recipe from Jana and Jeff Reboulet. The original recipe called for ground beef and Romano cheese. I substituted lean ground turkey and Parmesan cheese, and chose other low sodium ingredients. For those of us who especially enjoy Italian food, this is a good low sodium alternative. Hint: Cook the manicotti shells for 1 minute less than package instructions. Shells are easier to stuff when they're not too soft.

1 T. basil olive oil
1 lb. extra lean ground turkey
1 small onion, chopped
1 egg
¼ c. Parmesan cheese
¼ c. low sodium bread crumbs
1. T. dried parsley
¼ t. Italian seasoning
¼ t. oregano
¼ t. basil
¼ t. pepper
8 manicotti shells, cooked 1 minute less than indicated on package
1 (24 oz) jar low sodium spaghetti sauce
½ c. low fat mozzarella cheese

Heat olive oil and sauté ground turkey and onion until turkey is no longer pink and onion is tender. Remove to mixing bowl. Add egg, cheese, bread crumbs, and seasonings to turkey and onion and mix well. Prepare a 9x13 pan with nonstick spray.

Cover bottom of the pan with 1/3 of the spaghetti sauce. Fill cooked manicotti shells with turkey mixture and place on top of sauce in pan. Cover with remaining sauce. Top with ½ c. low fat mozzarella cheese. Bake in 350 degree oven for 40 to 45 minutes.

Yield: 4 servings

Per serving (2 shells) = 174 calories, 4 g saturated fat, 135 mg cholesterol, 160 mg sodium

MEATLOAF WITH TOMATO SAUCE

This recipe was adapted from Essentia's Cardiac Rehab Center. For a low sodium dish, it is quite tasty.

1 lb. extra lean ground beef
1 egg
2 T. Penzey's red and green bell pepper or ¼ c. diced green pepper
¼ c. chopped onion
½ c. oatmeal
1 t. chili powder
1 T. Worcestershire sauce
¼ t. pepper
Sauce: 1 (16 oz) can no salt tomato sauce, 1 (5 oz) can low sodium V8 juice, 2 T. yellow or spicy brown mustard, 2 T. brown sugar, 1 ½ t. chili powder

Combine all ingredients (except sauce ingredients) and shape into loaf.

Mix sauce ingredients and cover meatloaf. Bake at 375 degrees for one hour in an uncovered pan.

Yield: 6 servings

Per serving = 220 calories, 10 g fat, 3 g saturated fat, 87 mg cholesterol, 150 mg sodium

MEXICAN LASAGNA

This south-of-the-border casserole is delicious. These days, we don't serve it as often as we did previously, as cottage cheese contains a fair amount of sodium. But we indulge once in a while, and when we are shopping for cottage cheese, we look for one with the lowest sodium and fat.

1 ½ lb. extra lean ground beef or ground turkey
1½ t. ground cumin
1 T. chili powder
¼ t. garlic powder
¼ t. red pepper
½ t. black pepper
1 (15 oz) can no salt diced tomatoes
10 to 12 (soft) corn tortillas
2 c. low sodium small curd cottage cheese, drained
1 c. low fat shredded cheddar cheese, divided
1 egg
Garnish: Shredded lettuce, chopped tomatoes, green onions, ½ c. reduced fat cheddar cheese

Brown beef or turkey; drain fat. Add spices and diced tomatoes; heat through. Cover bottom and sides of a 9x13 baking dish with tortillas. Pour beef or turkey mix over tortillas; place a layer of tortillas over meat mixture; set aside. Combine cottage cheese, 1 c. shredded cheddar cheese, and egg; pour over tortillas. Bake at 350 degrees for 40 minutes. Remove from oven and sprinkle rows of cheddar cheese, lettuce, tomatoes, and green onions diagonally across center of casserole.

Yield: 6 to 8 servings

Per serving = 214 calories, 3.5 g saturated fat, 119 mg cholesterol, 183 mg sodium

MOM'S CHOP SUEY

As a child, I enjoyed Mom's chop suey. Still do, but swap the soy sauce for the substitute (see recipe on page 41) and I use low sodium stir fry vegetables, as they have considerably less sodium than Chinese vegetables.

1 lb. appropriate beef (round steak, family steak, sirloin)
1 c. onion, chopped
2 T. molasses
4 T. soy sauce substitute
3 c. water
1 c. celery, chopped fine
1 (28 oz) can low sodium Chinese vegetables
1 (8 oz) can water chestnuts
1 (8 oz) can bamboo shoots
Pinch of ginger

Brown meat and onions; drain fat. Add molasses, soy sauce substitute, water and celery. Cover and simmer ¾ hour or longer. Add more water if necessary. Add Chinese vegetables, water chestnuts and bamboo shoots. Cover; simmer ½ hour longer. Thicken with cornstarch.

Yield: 6 servings

Per serving = 149 calories, 3 g saturated fat, 37 mg cholesterol, 215 mg sodium

MOM'S FAMOUS SPAGHETTI

I recall my mom told me she found this recipe in the local newspaper years and years ago. She added a few ingredients to the original recipe. My entire family would probably agree that Mom's/Grandma's spaghetti recipe is just the best ever! Okay, I'll admit I still make it the "original" way now and again for extended family, but usual and customary these days is without the pepperoni and salt, and with no salt tomatoes. Either way, still a keeper, and it reminds us of Mom.

2 (15 oz) cans no salt diced tomatoes plus 2 (15 oz) cans of water
2 (12 oz) cans tomato paste plus 3 (12 oz) cans of water
½ t. sugar
½ t. black pepper
½ t. basil
½ t. garlic powder
½ t. allspice
½ t. oregano
2 t. parsley
1 large green pepper, chopped
3 stalks of celery, chopped
1 large onion, chopped

In large pot, simmer 2 cans of tomatoes with 2 cans of water. Add spices and let cook. Sauté green pepper, celery and onion, and add to sauce. Add 2 cans of tomato paste with 3 cans of water and let sauce come to a boil. Add meatballs (following) to sauce (or Italian sausage). Simmer 2 to 3 hours. Add more water if sauce thickens too much.

Per 1 c. serving = 143 calories, 1 g saturated fat, 12 mg cholesterol, 57 mg sodium

MEATBALLS FOR MOM'S SPAGHETTI

Can't have Mom's Famous Spaghetti without the meatballs!

1 lb. lean ground beef
1 egg
½ t. Mrs. Dash Original Blend seasoning
1 small onion, chopped fine
1 c. low sodium bread crumbs
¼ t. black pepper
¼ t. allspice
1 ½ t. parsley
Water to soften

Roll mixture into balls, softening mixture with water as needed. Brown meatballs under broiler, turning once. Add to sauce. Makes approximately 20 meatballs.

Per serving (2 meatballs) = 83 calories, 2.5 g saturated fat, 105 mg cholesterol, 50 mg sodium

OREGANO LEMON CHICKEN

An easy-to-put-together chicken dish. Easy clean up, too.

6 chicken thighs
3 T. lemon juice
2 T. honey
1 T. olive oil
3 garlic cloves, minced
2 t. dried oregano

Prepare pan by spraying with non-stick cooking spray. Place chicken in pan. Combine lemon juice, honey, oil, garlic and oregano; pour over chicken. Bake at 375 degrees for 45 minutes, or until meat thermometer reads 180 degrees. Baste occasionally.

Per serving = 147 calories, 2 g saturated fat, 49 mg cholesterol, 45 mg sodium

ORZO SKILLET

This recipe is a decent vegetarian entrée. Makes a lot. This is stove-top prepared, but goes in the oven under the broiler for the last 5 minutes. So be sure to use a Dutch oven that is appropriate for your broiler!

1 lb. orzo
1 T. olive oil
1 yellow onion, diced
1 (2 lb) bag Mediterranean vegetables
½ t. minced garlic (2 cloves)
3 T. balsamic vinegar
1 (15 oz) can diced tomatoes with basil, garlic and oregano (no salt)
¼ t. crushed red pepper flakes
¼ c. Parmesan cheese, grated
¼ c. reduced fat mozzarella cheese, shredded
Cook orzo – reserve ½ c. cooking liquid

Sauté onion in olive oil. Add Mediterranean vegetables. Cook until softened. Add vinegar and tomatoes to skillet, season with garlic and red pepper flakes. Turn down heat for 1 to 2 minutes, and then add orzo and the ½ c. cooking liquid. Mix orzo with cooked vegetables, then smooth the mixture and cover with cheese. Preheat broiler. Place broiler-okay Dutch oven/skillet in oven about 5 minutes or until cheese melts and begins to brown.

Per 2 c. serving = 245 calories, 2 g saturated fat, 25 mg cholesterol, 240 mg sodium

OVEN BAKED CHICKEN TENDERS

Mrs. Dash and Italian seasonings provide flavor for this dish.

1 lb. pkg. chicken tenders
½ c. whole wheat flour
2 egg whites
1 c. Panko bread crumbs
½ t. Italian seasoning
1 t. Mrs. Dash Tomato Basil seasoning

Heat oven to 375 degrees. Prepare an assembly line of 2 plates and one cereal bowl. Place a cookie sheet (coated with cooking spray) at the end of the line. First in line is the flour. Place ½ c. whole wheat flour on the plate. Take egg whites and whisk in cereal bowl. In third place are bread crumbs and spices. Roll chicken in flour, dip in egg whites, and roll in bread crumbs, landing them on cookie sheet. Continue until all chicken is coated. Place in oven; bake 25 minutes or until golden brown.

Yield: 4 or 5 servings

Per serving = 108 calories, 1 g saturated fat, 67 mg cholesterol, 76 mg sodium

OVEN BAKED FAJITAS

This recipe was adapted from one that I found online. It has become a fast favorite! Be sure to bake it uncovered.

1 lb. chicken, cut into strips
2 t. chili powder
1 ½ t. cumin
½ t. garlic powder
½ t. oregano
¼ t. Mrs. Dash Original Blend seasoning
1 (15 oz) can no salt diced tomatoes, drained
1 (4 oz) can green chilies
1 medium onion, sliced
1 red pepper and 1 green pepper, cut into strips

Preheat oven to 400 degrees. Place chicken strips in 9x13 baking dish, coated with nonstick spray. Combine spices. Drizzle spices over chicken and stir to coat. Add drained tomatoes, green chilies, peppers and onions and stir to combine. Bake uncovered 25 to 30 minutes or until chicken is cooked through and peppers and onions are tender. Serve on tortillas with your choice of garnish.

Per serving (2 fajitas with 2/3 c. chicken, peppers and onions) = 299 calories, 0.5 g saturated fat, 31 mg cholesterol, 285 mg sodium

PARMESAN PECAN CHICKEN

This recipe is super easy, and it's low calorie, too!

½ c. fat free or low fat milk
1 ¼ c. low sodium bread crumbs
½ c. finely chopped pecans
¼ c. Parmesan cheese
3 t. basil
3. t. oregano
1 t. garlic powder
½ t. Italian seasoning
4 boneless skinless chicken breasts
2 t. canola oil

Place milk in a shallow bowl. In a separate bowl, combine bread crumbs, pecans, cheese and seasonings. Dip chicken in milk; roll in crumb mixture. In a nonstick skillet, brown chicken in oil. Transfer chicken to a baking sheet that has been coated with nonstick cooking spray. Bake uncovered at 350 degrees for 30 minutes or until a meat thermometer reads 170 degrees.

Yield: 4 servings

Per serving = 229 calories, 2 g saturated fat, 65 mg cholesterol, 143 mg sodium

PIZZA SAUCE

This recipe was adapted from one from Essentia Health's Cardiac Rehab Center. Add tomatoes thinly sliced with basil olive oil for a delicious pizza topping and a good alternative to pepperoni.

2 t. basil olive oil
¼ c. onion, finely chopped
¼ c. green pepper, finely chopped (or use equivalent Penzey's red and green bell pepper)
1/8 t. garlic powder
½ t. sugar
½ t. Italian seasoning
1 t. oregano
1 t. dried basil
¼ t. pepper
1 (8 oz) can no salt tomato sauce
2 t. tomato paste

In medium saucepan, sauté onion and green pepper in olive oil under tender. Add the seasonings and continue cooking a few more minutes. Stir in tomato sauce and then tomato paste. Simmer on low heat for about 10 minutes.

Per 2 T. serving = 33 calories, 0 g saturated fat, 0 cholesterol, 5 mg sodium

POLYNESIAN MEATBALLS

These meatballs can be made with either ground beef or ground turkey. Years ago Becky, a coworker, made them for a potluck, and I asked for the recipe. I eliminated the soy sauce and spices with salt and came up with a tasty alternative. Meatballs can be made small and used as an appetizer, or larger size meatballs make for a tasty dinner.

Meatballs:
1 ½ pounds ground beef or turkey
2/3 c. oatmeal
1 (8 oz) can water chestnuts, drained and finely chopped
½ c. low fat milk
1 T. soy sauce substitute (see condiments, page 41)
1 egg
½ t. onion powder
½ t. garlic powder

Combine all meatball ingredients. Shape into small balls. If mixture is too wet, add more oatmeal. Bake meatballs on a baking pan (coated with cooking spray) in a 350 degree oven for about 40 minutes.

Sauce:
1 (5 oz) can crushed pineapple (or pineapple tidbits)
1 c. brown sugar
3 T. cornstarch
½ c. cider vinegar
2 T. soy sauce substitute (see condiment section)
1 c. unsalted beef stock or low sodium beef bouillon

Drain pineapple, reserving juice. In medium saucepan, combine brown sugar and cornstarch, stir in pineapple juice, beef stock or bouillon, vinegar and soy sauce substitute. Heat to boiling, stirring constantly, until thick and clear. Boil for about a minute. Stir in pineapple. Add sauce to meatballs.

Per serving (3 dinner-sized meatballs) = 93 calories, 1 g saturated fat, 19 mg cholesterol, 182 mg sodium

👑

SLOPPY JOES WITH RED LENTILS

This was adapted from a recipe from Essentia Health's Cardiac Rehab Center. We needed more "zip," so added chili powder. We actually prefer using extra lean ground turkey. Add a multi grain bun, vegetable, and baked basil wedges (see page 76), and dinner is served!

1 lb. extra lean ground beef or ground turkey
1 large onion, chopped
½ c. water
1 (8 oz) can no salt tomato sauce
½ c. red lentils, rinsed
½ c. low sodium ketchup
1 t. apple cider vinegar
1 T. sugar or Splenda
½ t. garlic powder
½ t. dry mustard
¼ t. pepper
¼ t. red pepper
1 T. chili powder

In large skillet or Dutch oven, cook beef or turkey and onion until meat is no longer pink; drain grease.   Add remaining ingredients. Bring to a boil. Reduce heat; cover and simmer for one hour or until lentils are tender. Add more water as needed for desired consistency.

Yield: 8 servings

Per serving with ground turkey = 145 calories, 1 g fat, 0.25 saturated fat, 35 mg cholesterol, 125 mg sodium. Per serving with ground beef = 175 calories, 6 g fat, 2 g saturated fat, 40 mg cholesterol, 130 mg sodium. (If you use regular ketchup and tomato sauce, sodium would increase to 410 mg per serving).

SLOPPY JOES TWO

The first sloppy joe recipe was with lentils; this one without. It is the more traditional recipe, but without the condensed chicken gumbo soup Mom used throughout the years. Still, it is quite tasty...and a quick meal.

1 ½ lbs. extra lean ground beef
1 onion, chopped
1 c. low sodium ketchup
1 green pepper, chopped
2 T. brown sugar
½ t. garlic powder
2 T. spicy brown mustard
3 T. cider vinegar
1 T. Worcestershire sauce
1 ½ t. chili powder

In large skillet, brown beef and onion. Drain fat. Stir together remaining ingredients. Cook until heated through, or place in slow cooker and cook on high for 3 hours, or low for 6 hours.

Yield: 8 servings

Per serving: 278 calories, 3 g saturated fat, 69 mg cholesterol, 77 mg sodium

SLOW COOKER CAJUN CHICKEN BREASTS

This recipe was clipped from a Duluth News Tribune recipe column many years ago. It's pretty spicy, so I adjusted the spices a bit. Heat it up or tone it down to your taste.

6 chicken breasts, boneless and skinless
1 (15 oz) can no salt diced tomatoes with basil, oregano and garlic
1 (6 oz) can tomato paste
½ c. white wine, if desired
½ c. chopped celery
½ c. chopped green pepper
1 T. minced onion
¼ t. red pepper flakes
½ t. black pepper
¼ t. white pepper
½ t. oregano
½ t. thyme
½ t. basil
½ t. garlic powder

Place chicken breasts in slow cooker. Combine diced tomatoes, tomato paste, celery, green pepper, onion and spices and pour over chicken. Cover and cook on low for 7 to 9 hours or high for 4 to 5 hours.

Yield: 6 servings

Per serving = 205 calories, 1 g saturated fat, 55 mg cholesterol, 79 mg sodium

SLOW COOKER CRANBERRY PORK

This is a good Sunday dinner recipe. We have also served it during the holidays. And best of all, it is easy, easy, easy! Recipe came from "Lickety-Split Meals" by Zonya Foco, RD, via Essentia's Cardiac Rehab Center.

8 hours before serving, place in slow cooker
2 ½ to 3 b. pork tenderloin or pork roast
In a medium bowl mix together
1 (16 oz) can whole berry jellied cranberry sauce, mashed
½ c. sugar or Splenda
½ c. light cranberry juice
1 t. dry mustard
¼ t. ground cloves

Dash of allspice

Pour over meat and cook on low for 8 hours or on high for 4 hours.

When pork is done, remove from slow cooker and lightly cover with aluminum foil.

Reserve cranberry mixture and pour into a pan. Whisk 2 T. cornstarch and 2 T. water and pour into cranberry mixture. Cook 1 minute until thick and bubbly.

Serve with mashed potatoes or egg noodles.

Per 4 oz serving of pork and ¼ c. gravy = 350 calories, 8 g fat, 2.5 g saturated fat, 143 mg cholesterol, 110 mg sodium

SOUTHWEST CHIPOTLE PORK CHOPS

*This recipe is a variation of one from Essentia Health's
Cardiac Rehab Center, adjusting spices and using Mrs. Dash's
Southwest Chipotle seasoning. It's got some heat, so feel free to
reduce the spice a bit. You can always add more!*

2 T. olive oil
4 pork loin chops
¼ c. red pepper, chopped
¼ c. green pepper, chopped
1 medium onion, chopped
1 (15 oz) can no salt diced tomatoes
1 c. frozen corn
1 (15 oz) can low sodium red kidney beans, rinsed and drained
½ c. long grain rice
1 t. chili powder
1 t. cumin
1 t. Mrs. Dash Southwest Chipotle seasoning
Optional: 1 Jalapeno pepper

Heat olive oil in skillet and brown chops on both sides. Set
chops aside; reserve drippings in skillet. Cook peppers and
onions in reserved drippings until tender. Stir in tomatoes,
corn, beans, uncooked rice and seasonings. Bring to boil. Place
mixture in baking dish coated with nonstick spray. Arrange
pork chops on top. Cover and bake in a 350 degree oven for 35
minutes. If desired, sprinkle with 1 seeded and finely chopped

Jalapeno pepper. Uncover and bake 10 to 15 minutes additional or until meat is tender.

Yield: 4 servings

Per serving with 1 ½ c. rice mixture and 1 pork chop = 474 calories, 16 g fat, 3.5 g saturated fat, 76 mg cholesterol, 173 mg sodium

SOUTHWESTERN PULLED PORK

Find the lowest sodium bottled barbecue sauce at the grocery store or make your own (page 39). Add a few kitchen staples for this easily prepared and one-pot to-clean-up dish. This pork is good either served on tortillas or multi-grain buns. A favorite of son David's.

2 (4 oz each) cans diced green chilies
1 (8 oz) can tomato sauce
1 c. low sodium barbeque sauce
1 large onion, chopped
¼ c. chili powder
1 t. cumin
1 t. oregano
¼ t. garlic powder
2 drops Tabasco sauce
2 ½ to 3 lb. pork loin roast

In a 3 qt. slow cooker, combine above ingredients. Add pork, cover, and cook on low for 8 hours or until meat is tender. Remove pork. When cool enough to handle, shred meat using two forks. Return to slow cooker and heat through.

Per 1 c. serving = 268 calories, 3 g saturated fat, 88 mg cholesterol, 137 mg sodium

TACO CASSEROLE

This is a variation of Mexican Lasagna, but this one has kidney beans.

1 lb. extra lean ground beef
1 onion, chopped
1 green pepper, chopped
¼ t. garlic powder
1 T. chili powder
½ t. oregano
½ t. cumin
1 (15 oz) can no salt diced tomatoes
1 (8 oz) can no salt tomato sauce
1 (15 oz) can low sodium kidney beans
12 (soft) corn tortillas
¾ c. shredded Swiss cheese

Brown ground beef, sauté onion and green pepper; drain fat. Add diced tomatoes, tomato sauce and spices; simmer 2 minutes. Place a layer of 4 tortillas in the bottom of a 9x13 baking pan sprayed with cooking spray. Place a layer of beef mixture over the top, then 4 more tortillas, the beans, the final 4 tortillas, and the rest of the beef mixture.

Bake at 350 degrees for 40 minutes. Sprinkle with cheese and return to oven until cheese is melted.

Yield: 6 large servings

Per serving = 368 calories, 3 g saturated fat, 61 mg cholesterol, 105 mg sodium

TEX MEX PORK CHOPS

A bit of a kick with salsa, these pork chops are a favorite of Jeff's.

1 small onion, chopped
6 boneless pork chops
1 c. low sodium salsa
1 (4 oz) can chopped green chilies
¼ c. green pepper
½ t. cumin
¼ t. black pepper

In a large skillet coated with nonstick spray, sauté onion until tender. Add pork chops and brown on each side. Place pork chops in a 9x13 pan coated with nonstick spray. Combine salsa, chilies, green pepper, cumin and black pepper, pour over pork. Bake at 350 degrees for 45 minutes or until a meat thermometer reads 160 degrees.

Yield: 6 servings

Per serving = 223 calories, 8 g fat, 3 g saturated fat, 68 mg cholesterol, 103 mg sodium

UPSIDE DOWN PIZZA

A family favorite, and super easy to put together. Another recipe of mom's.

1 lb. extra lean ground beef or turkey
1 medium onion, chopped
1 (16 oz) jar of low sodium spaghetti sauce
½ lb. Italian sausage (see page 113), green pepper, mushrooms, or desired vegetable toppings
1 c. low fat mozzarella cheese
2 eggs
1 c. low fat milk
1 T. canola oil
1 c. flour
¼ t. salt
Parmesan cheese

Brown beef or turkey with onion in large skillet; drain fat. Add spaghetti sauce to beef or turkey and mix together. Place mixture in a 9x13 pan that has been coated with nonstick spray. Add toppings as desired. Sprinkle with mozzarella cheese. Beat 2 eggs, milk, oil, flour and salt. Pour egg mixture over mozzarella cheese. Sprinkle Parmesan cheese on top. Bake at 400 degrees for 30 minutes.

Yield: 6 generous servings

Per serving = 279 calories, 2 g saturated fat, 43 mg cholesterol, 265 mg sodium

VEGETABLE PIZZA WITH CAULIFLOWER CRUST

I found this recipe on a fitness website. I revised it to add more vegetables and reduced the cheese a bit. Variations include adding low sodium sun dried tomatoes, spinach, roasted peppers and onions, sliced tomatoes sprinkled with basil, and even Italian sausage (see page 113). It's a great way to get more vegetables in with a delicious pizza taste. Low calorie, too! You can't pick this pizza up—you will need a fork to enjoy every bite! Delicious and nutritious!

½ large head of fresh cauliflower (preferred) or 16. oz. package of frozen cauliflower florets
1 egg
½ c. shredded reduced fat cheddar cheese
1 t. oregano
2 t. basil
¼ t. dried Italian seasoning (no salt)
1/8 t. pepper
1 (15 oz) jar low sodium pizza or pasta sauce
Pizza toppings: Desired fresh, chopped vegetables (such as mushrooms, onions, green peppers, spinach)
¼ c. shredded reduced fat mozzarella cheese

Break apart cauliflower and cut into florets. Roast in a 400 degree oven until tender, about 15 minutes.

Finely chop the roasted cauliflower, or use a food processor or ricer. Mix cauliflower, egg, shredded cheddar cheese, basil and oregano and pepper. Press mixture into a pizza pan that has been sprayed with non-stick spray. Bake for 15 minutes.

Remove from oven and add low sodium pizza sauce (we like Enrico's), low fat mozzarella cheese, Italian seasoning, and your favorite vegetables. Return to oven and bake 9 minutes or until cheese melts.

Per serving (1/2 pizza) = 175 calories, 8 g fat, 3 g saturated fat, 105 mg cholesterol, 310 mg sodium

UNCLE DICK'S LASAGNA

The relatives always raved about Uncle Dick's lasagna. This one is modified a bit from the original. Okay to splurge now and again.

2 large onions, chopped
1 or 2 garlic gloves, minced
1 green pepper
3 stalks of celery
1 lb. extra lean ground beef
1 lb. Italian sausage (see page 113)
1 (28 oz) can no salt plum tomatoes
2 (8 oz) cans no salt tomato sauce
2 (6 oz) cans tomato paste
1 (5 oz) can low sodium V8 juice
1/8 t. salt
¼ t. pepper
½ t. sugar
1 t. oregano
1 lb. lasagna noodles
1 (8 oz) pkg. low fat mozzarella cheese and (2 T.) Parmesan cheese

Finely chop vegetables and sauté in Dutch oven that has been coated with nonstick cooking spray. Brown ground beef and Italian sausage in Dutch oven. Drain fat. Add tomatoes, tomato sauce, tomato paste, V8 juice, seasonings and sugar. Bring to boil; simmer sauce 3 to 4 hours.

Cook lasagna noodles in large pot. Drain; place noodles between layers of wax paper, and set aside to cool. Ladle sauce to cover the bottom of a 9x13 baking pan prepared with nonstick spray. Then layer lasagna noodles, then mozzarella cheese, then more sauce, alternating layers until pan is full. Sprinkle Parmesan cheese on top. Bake covered for 45 minutes in a 350 degree oven. Remove from oven and let set for 10 minutes before serving. Yield: 6 to 8 servings.

Per serving = 315 calories, 3.5 g saturated fat, 117 mg cholesterol, 166 mg sodium

VEGETABLE LASAGNA

I developed this recipe when I didn't want to chop a lot of vegetables. Even shared this one with Tom, our favorite Schwan's delivery man!

1 (2 lb) bag Schwan's Mediterranean Vegetable Blend
1 c. low fat cottage cheese AND 2/3 c. low fat shredded Swiss cheese
OR
1 tub fat free Ricotta cheese and 2/3 c. low fat mozzarella cheese

2 eggs
1 ½ t. Italian Seasoning (no salt)
1/8 t. black pepper
12 lasagna noodles, cooked
2 to 3 c. low sodium marinara sauce
½ c. shredded Swiss cheese
¼ c/ grated Parmesan cheese

To assemble: Place a little sauce on the bottom of a 9x13 baking dish, sprayed with olive oil cooking spray. Place 3 noodles on top of sauce. Add layer of vegetables and a layer of cheese mixture. Add more sauce. Repeat. For last layer, sprinkle sauce and then low fat Swiss cheese. Sprinkle with low fat Parmesan cheese on top. Bake in 350 degree oven for 45 minutes or until bubbly.

Yield: 6 to 8 servings.

Per serving = 269 calories, 4 g saturated fat, 30, mg cholesterol, 310 mg sodium

WHITE HOUSE TURKEY LASAGNA WITH SPINACH – REVISED

I found this recipe while surfing the Internet. First Lady Michelle Obama apparently said this recipe was among favorites of the First Family. It was pretty "healthy" already, but I managed to skinny it down a bit more. It takes a bit of time to make, but it is well worth it....it's delicious!

1 T. basil olive oil
1 c. chopped yellow onion
½ t. minced garlic (or 3 cloves garlic)
1 lb. extra lean ground turkey
1 (28 oz) can plum tomatoes, crushed (low sodium)
1 (6 oz) can tomato paste
¼ t. pepper
1 T. fresh basil (or about 2 t. dried)
1 T. fresh parsley (1 ½ t. dried)
1 t. dried Italian seasoning (no salt)
1 (15 oz) tub fat free ricotta cheese
¾ c. Parmesan cheese
1 egg
2 lbs. fresh spinach, washed, but not dried
16 lasagna noodles, cooked
1 lb. reduced fat mozzarella cheese

Preheat oven to 400 degrees. In a Dutch oven, add 1 T. basil olive oil, add onion and cook until translucent. Add garlic and cook additional minute. Add ground turkey and cook 10 minutes or until no longer pink. Add crushed tomatoes, tomato paste and pepper; simmer until thickened, about 20 minutes. Stir in basil, parsley and Italian seasoning. Set aside. Combine ricotta, ½ c. Parmesan cheese and egg, season with pepper; set aside. Place damp spinach in large skillet over medium heat and cook until wilted. Prepare a 9x13 pan with nonstick spray. Layer in turkey mix, noodles, mozzarella, ricotta mixture, and spinach. Repeat layers 2 more times. Sprinkle mozzarella and parmesan cheeses on top. Bake until bubbly, about 30 minutes. Yield: 6 to 8 servings.

Per serving = 347 calories, 4 g saturated fat, 78 mg cholesterol, 372 mg sodium

Sweet Endings

ALMOND SHORTBREAD THUMBPRINTS

This recipe came from a good friend and former colleague.
Decorative and delicious! Fun for Valentine's Day.

2/3 c. sugar or 1/3 c. sugar and 1/3 c. Splenda
1 c. unsalted butter
¾ t. almond extract
¼ t. vanilla extract
2. c. flour
½ c. raspberry jam (or your favorite jam)
Glaze: 1 c. powdered sugar, 1 ½ t. almond extract, and 2 to 3 t. water

Heat oven to 350 degrees. Beat sugar, butter and extracts until creamy. Add flour and continue beating until well mixed. Shape dough into small balls. Depress with thumb and fill each indentation with a small amount of jam. Bake 14 minutes or until lightly browned on edges.

Make glaze by adding water until it is thin enough to drizzle. Criss cross glaze over cookies once they have cooled. Be sure to let glaze harden before stacking and storing cookies.

Per serving (2 cookies) = 108 calories, 3 g saturated fat, 25 mg cholesterol, 86 mg sodium

APPLE CRANBERRY CRISP

A variation of regular apple crisp. Experiment with other fruits such as rhubarb and strawberries or raspberries or your favorite combination.

5 c. apples, peeled and chopped
2 c. cranberries
1 c. Splenda or sugar
1 ½ T. cornstarch
Topping: ½ c. flour, 1/3 c. old fashioned oatmeal, ½ c. brown sugar, ½ t. cinnamon, 2 T. tub margarine

Preheat oven to 350 degrees. Lightly spray 9x11 pan with cooking spray.

In large bowl toss fruit with Splenda or sugar and cornstarch. Pour into pan.

In small bowl, combine oatmeal, flour, brown sugar and cinnamon. Cut in margarine. Mix until crumbly. Spread over fruit.

Bake 45 minutes or until bubbly.

Per ½ c. serving with Splenda = 85 calories, 0 g saturated fat, 0 cholesterol, 20 mg sodium

CHERRY COBBLER CRUMBLE

Quick and easy. Serve with nonfat whipped topping for a yummy treat.

1 can low sugar cherry pie filling
2 T. unsalted tub margarine
½ c. quick oatmeal
¼ c. flour
½ c. sugar or Splenda
2 T. chopped pecans or walnuts

Spray 8 inch square pan with baking spray. Pour cherry pie filling into pan. Mix margarine, oatmeal, flour, sugar or Splenda, and nuts. Crumble over pie filling. Bake 350 degrees for 20 to 25 minutes.

Per serving = 150 calories, 2 g saturated fat, 0 mg cholesterol, 24 mg sodium

CHERRY OAT SQUARES

This recipe was stuck on a can of Wilderness Cherry Pie filling years and years ago.

1/3 c. sugar or Splenda
1 c. chopped walnuts or pecans
1 c. old fashioned oatmeal
½ c. light margarine or butter, softened
¾ c. all-purpose flour
½ t. cinnamon
1/8 t. nutmeg
1 (20 oz) can light cherry pie filling

Preheat oven to 400 degrees. Mix sugar, nuts, oatmeal, margarine or butter and flour until crumbly. Reserve about 1 ½ cups. Press remainder in bottom of 8 inch square baking dish, sprayed with nonstick spray. Stir cinnamon and nutmeg into cherry filling. Spread over crust. Sprinkle reserved crumbs over top, pressing in lightly. Bake for 25 minutes or until lightly browned.

Per serving = 150 calories, 2 g saturated fat, 10 mg cholesterol, 118 mg sodium

CHEWY OATMEAL DROP COOKIES

This was one of the first recipes I tried that was low fat, low sodium. It was early on in our healthy eating journey, and I recall sitting at the computer for hours, trying to find suitable recipes. It's not an overly sweet cookie. It doesn't make a lot, so the cookie jar doesn't stay filled very long!

1/3 c. canola oil
1/3 c. brown sugar
2 T. sugar
3 T. water
1 egg white
¾ t. vanilla extract
1/3 c. all-purpose flour
1/3 c. whole wheat flour
2. t. cinnamon
½ t. baking soda
¼ t. salt
2 c. old-fashioned oatmeal
½ c. raisins or dried cranberries

Combine oil, sugars, water, egg white and vanilla in large bowl. Combine dry ingredients and gradually add to sugar mixture and mix well. Stir in oats and raisins or cranberries.

Drop by scant ¼ cupfuls onto baking sheets coated with cooking spray. Flatten slightly. Bake for 10 to 12 minutes until golden brown at 350 degrees.

Per serving (2 cookies) = 144 calories, 1 g saturated fat, 0 cholesterol, 86 mg sodium

CHOCOLATE OATMEAL CAKE

Similar to Mom's Westhaven bars, but with oatmeal. This recipe was an Essentia Heart Cardiac Rehab Center goodie.

1 c. oatmeal
1 ½ c. boiling water
¾ c. granulated sugar
¾ c. light brown sugar
1/3 c. canola oil
4 egg whites
½ c. cocoa powder
1 ½ c. flour
1 t. baking soda
¼ t. salt
1 t. vanilla extract
½ t. almond extract
½ c. chopped nuts (pecans, walnuts, or almonds)
½ c. dark chocolate chips

Preheat oven to 350 degrees.

Pour boiling water over oatmeal and set aside. Combine sugars and oil. Beat egg whites lightly and add to sugar and oil mixture. Combine dry ingredients. Add dry ingredients to oil mixture. Combine but don't overbeat. Add extracts and stir. Add oatmeal to batter. Pour into 9x13 pan sprayed with nonstick baking spray. Top with nuts and chocolate chips. Bake 30 to 35 minutes or until toothpick inserted in center comes out clean.

Per serving = 167 calories, 0.5 g saturated fat, 0 cholesterol, 120 mg sodium

CINNAMON CRANBERRY OAT ENERGY BARS

These bars can be used as a breakfast bar or just a good energy treat. I found a variation of this recipe in a Taste of Home magazine, but it was too crumbly. A few adjustments and I think it is pretty good.

3 c. quick oatmeal
1 ¾ c. Rice Krispies
1 ¼ c. dried cranberries
½ c. ground flaxseed
1/3 c. walnuts
1 t. cinnamon
½ t. nutmeg
½ c. brown sugar
½ c. light corn syrup
¼ c. canola oil
¼ c. honey
1 t. vanilla extract
2 t. sugar plus ¼ t. cinnamon

In large bowl combine oats, Rice Krispies, cranberries, flax, walnuts, 1 t. cinnamon and nutmeg.

In a large saucepan, combine brown sugar, corn syrup, oil and honey; cook and stir over medium heat until sugar is dissolved. Remove from heat; stir in vanilla.

Stir in oat mixture; toss to coat. Press firmly into a 9x12 in. pan coated with cooking spray. Combine cinnamon and sugar; sprinkle over bars. Cool completely and cut into bars.

Per serving – 211 calories, 6 g fat, trace saturated fat, 0 cholesterol, 72 mg sodium

CRANBERRY CAKE

This recipe originally came from my Aunt Bev. I clipped a variation from the local newspaper from a "People's Choice Award" winner in a recipe contest. I reduced sugar, used light tub margarine, and changed the cream in the caramel sauce to fat free evaporated milk. Yummy!

3 T. light tub margarine
½ c. sugar
½ c. Splenda
2 c. flour
1 c. low fat milk
2 t. baking powder
¼ t. salt
3 c. fresh (raw) cranberries

Beat all ingredients together and fold in cranberries. Pour into 8 or 9 inch square baking pan coated with nonstick spray. Bake at 350 degrees for 35 minutes or until top is brown. Serve warm or cold with caramel sauce.

Per serving = 200 calories, 2 g saturated fat, 45 mg cholesterol, 113 mg sodium

CARAMEL SAUCE

½ c. light tub margarine
½ c. fat free evaporated milk
½ c. sugar
½ c. Splenda
1 t. vanilla or almond extract

In a saucepan, bring all ingredients except extract to a boil over medium heat, stirring constantly. Turn heat way down. Add vanilla or almond extract. Serve warm sauce over cranberry cake.

Per serving = 86 calories, 1.5 g saturated fat, 30 mg cholesterol, 65 mg sodium

CRANBERRY NUT BISCOTTI

This is my favorite sweet.....Jeff's too, I think. I like cranberry pistachio the best, but the main recipe can be changed to just about any flavor you like. One batch is about 2 dozen biscotti. I make biscotti for gifts, or "just because." During one holiday baking episode, I lost a small ruby in my dough. Never found it, and I am not aware of any complaints or broken teeth as a result!

3/4 c. sugar
¼ c. canola oil
2 eggs
2 t. vanilla extract
1 t. almond extract
1 ¾ c. all-purpose flour
1 t. baking powder
¼ t. salt
2/3 c. chopped nuts (pistachios, walnuts, pecans, almonds)
½ c. dried cranberries

In a bowl, beat sugar and oil until blended. Beat in eggs, then extracts. Combine dry ingredients; gradually add to sugar mixture and mix well (dough will be stiff). Stir in nuts and cranberries.

Divide dough in half. With floured hands, shape each half into a 12x 3 inch rectangle on a wax paper lined baking sheet. Bake at 350 degrees for about 19 or 20 minutes or until set.

When cool enough to handle, transfer biscotti to a cutting board; cut (at a diagonal) with a serrated knife into ¾ inch slices. Place on ungreased baking sheet. Bake 7 minutes; turn biscotti slices over and bake for another 6 to 7 minutes or until firm. (If using dark color baking sheets, reduce time a couple of minutes). Cool on wire racks. Store in airtight container.

Variations:

Orange Cranberry Pistachio (Trader Joes's dried orange cranberries + 2 t. orange peel or orange zest and pistachios), Chocolate Chip Walnut (add mini chocolate chips and walnuts), Apricot Almond (dried apricot pieces and sliced almonds).

Per serving (1 biscotti) = 85 calories, 3 g fat (trace saturated fat) 13 mg cholesterol, 46 mg sodium

DARK CHOCOLATE RASPBERRY CAKE

This one is compliments of the Essential Health Wellness Program. It is my "to go to" cake for Valentine's Day (but delicious for any other day, too)! Yield: 18 small pieces.

1 c. quick oatmeal
1 c. boiling water
½ c. evaporated fat free milk
1 T. white vinegar
½ c. white sugar
½ c. brown sugar
1/3 c. canola oil
2 eggs
2 egg whites
½ c. cocoa powder
½ c. all-purpose flour
1 c. whole wheat flour
½ t. baking soda
½ t. baking powder
1 t. vanilla extract
½ t. almond extract
10 oz. frozen raspberries
½ c. chopped nuts (walnuts or pecans)

Preheat oven to 350 degrees. Pour boiling water over oatmeal and set aside to cool, and then stir in evaporated milk and vinegar. Beat sugars and oil until smooth. Whisk eggs and egg whites in a small bowl. Add to sugar and oil mixture. Combine dry ingredients. Add dry mixture to oil mixture. Stir together, but don't overbeat. Add extracts and stir. Add oatmeal mixture and frozen raspberries to batter, and mix until just combined.

Pour into a 9x13 pan coated with nonstick baking spray. Top with chopped nuts and bake for 35 to 40 minutes or until a toothpick inserted in center comes out clean.

Per serving = 165 calories, 5 g fat, 0.5 g saturated fat, 20 mg cholesterol, 75 mg sodium

DARK CHOCOLATE SAUCE

Tastes great on low fat, no sugar vanilla ice cream....Really!
We make this often. Okay I admit it. When I am really
desperate for chocolate, I might just have a tablespoon of this
all by itself!

1 c. brown sugar
1 c. cocoa
2 T. cornstarch
1 c. low or fat free milk
½ c. strong brewed coffee
2 t. vanilla extract
1 t. almond extract

In large saucepan, combine brown sugar, cocoa and cornstarch.
Stir in milk and coffee until smooth. Bring to boil; cook and stir
for 1 to 2 minutes or until thickened. Stir in extracts. Add more
milk or coffee if it gets too thick. Store in refrigerator.

Note: experiment with flavored coffee for an extra special treat.

Per 2 T. serving = 77 calories, 1 g saturated fat, 1 mg cholesterol, 16 mg sodium

FAT-FREE CHOCOLATE THERAPY CAKE

Found this recipe years and years ago in the Duluth News Tribune. Frost with my chocolate frosting, next page.

6 egg whites
¾ c. sugar or Splenda
1 T. vanilla extract
¾ c. flour
1/3 c. cocoa
¼ t. salt
1 t. baking powder
1 ½ c. (7 oz tub) marshmallow creme

Add ingredients one at a time into medium bowl, stirring well after each addition. Add marshmallow creme and mix until the lumps are gone. Pour into a 9 inch pan that has been coated with nonstick baking spray. Bake at 325 degrees for 35 to 40 minutes, or until toothpick inserted in center comes out clean.

Makes 10 small servings at less than ½ g fat each.

Per serving = 140 calories, 119 mg sodium

EASY CHOCOLATE FROSTING

1 c. powdered sugar
¼ c. unsweetened cocoa powder
2 T. low fat milk (or 2 T. brewed coffee)
¼ t. almond extract
1 (8 oz) tub fat free whipped topping, thawed
Chopped pecans or walnuts (optional)

In medium bowl, stir all ingredients except whipped topping. Gently fold in whipped topping. Frost cake. Sprinkle with unsalted chopped pecans or walnuts if desired.

Per 2 T. serving = 45 calories, 0 fat, 0 cholesterol, 7 mg sodium

FLUFFY KEY LIME PIE

I love the tastes and smells of anything citrus. This key lime pie is a light, low fat delight. Garnish with lime slices, if desired.

1 (3 oz) package sugar free lime Jell-O
¼ c. boiling water
2 cartons (6 oz each) low fat key lime yogurt
1 carton (8 oz) fat free whipped topping, thawed
1 reduced fat graham cracker crust

Dissolve Jell-O in boiling water. Whisk in yogurt. Fold in whipped topping. Pour into crust. Cover and refrigerate until set or at least 2 hours.

Yield: 8 servings

Per serving = 194 calories, 3 g fat, 1 g saturated fat, 2 mg cholesterol, 159 mg sodium

FRESH APPLE "DUMP" CAKE

I'm not sure where this recipe came from, but I sure like it. To make it heart healthier than the original recipe, I reduced the salt, added whole wheat flour, Splenda and dates. Best of all, it is easy....just "dump" ingredients in one bowl. The cake is especially good at Fall Harvest time when apples are tasty and abundant. We enjoy this cake with fat free whipped topping or low sugar, low fat ice cream.

4 c. peeled diced apples
1 c. sugar
1 c. Splenda
½ c. chopped walnuts
½ c. chopped dates
1 c. canola oil
2 eggs or equivalent in egg substitute
1 ¼ t. vanilla extract

Put apples in large mixing bowl. Add sugar and Splenda, oil, nuts and dates and mix thoroughly.

Add eggs and vanilla extract and combine. Then "dump in" the rest of ingredients:

1 t. baking soda
2 t. cinnamon
½ t. nutmeg
½ t. salt
1 c. all-purpose flour
1 c. whole wheat flour

Stir mixture and place in 9x13 cake pan that has been sprayed generously with baking spray. Bake at 325 degrees for 55 minutes to 1 hour or until toothpick inserted in center comes out clean.

Per serving = 211 calories, 1 g saturated fat, 31 mg cholesterol, 70 mg sodium

FRUIT PIZZA

A long-ago work potluck was where I came across this goodie. Jen was kind enough to share the recipe. Modified a bit for lower fat and sugar content. This is good to make the night before and serve the next day. It tastes as good as it looks!

½ c. powdered sugar
1 c. all-purpose flour
½ c. whole wheat flour
¾ c. unsalted butter

Mix together; bake crust at 350 degrees for 15 to 20 minutes.

8 oz. reduced fat cream cheese
½ c. sugar
½ c. Splenda
1 ¼ t. vanilla

Mix together; put filling on cooled crust.

Fruit for pizza:
1 (20 oz) can crushed pineapple (drain, but save juice)
Apple, banana, grapes, strawberries, raspberries, blueberries, cantaloupe, kiwi or your favorite fruits.

Mix all fruit together. Drain and save juice. Put fruit over filling.

Glaze

Mix fruit juice, pineapple juice and water necessary to equal 1 ½ cups.

Add:

1 c. sugar (or combination of sugar and Splenda)
4 T. cornstarch
3 T. light corn syrup

Boil until clear, 10 to 15 minutes. Cool glaze; pour over fruit mixture. Refrigerate.

Per serving = 163 calories, 2.5 g fat, 0 cholesterol, 32 mg sodium

LIGHTENED-UP HOLIDAY COOKIE DOUGH

The holidays can be a struggle when you are trying to limit fat and sodium. This versatile cookie dough can be the base for other cookies as well as used for your cutouts. And with 1 gram of saturated fat, 39 mg of sodium and at only 56 calories, it's okay to have 2! This one courtesy of Taste of Home archives.

1 c. unsalted butter, softened
1 c. sugar
½ c. Splenda
1 ½ c. brown sugar
3 eggs or equivalent in egg substitute
1/3 c. canola oil
1 ½ t. vanilla extract
½ t. almond extract
4 c. flour
½ t. salt
½ t. baking soda

In a large bowl, cream butter, sugars and Splenda until light and fluffy. Beat in eggs or egg substitute, oil and extracts. Combine flour, salt and soda; gradually add to creamed mixture and mix well.

Divide dough into four portions. Shape each into a ball; wrap each individually in plastic wrap. Refrigerate for 1 hour or until easy to handle, or freeze up to 3 months.

To use refrigerated cookie dough: Divide each portion into 2 balls; roll each ball directly onto an ungreased baking sheet to ¼ inch thickness. Cut with a floured cookie cutter, leaving at least 1 inch between cookies. Remove excess dough and reroll scraps.

Bake at 350 degrees for 6 to 7 minutes or until bottoms are lightly browned. Cool for 2 minutes before removing to wire racks to cool completely. Decorate as desired.

To use frozen dough: Thaw in the refrigerator overnight. Bake according to recipe directions above.

Yield: 10 dozen cookies

Per serving (1 cookie) = 56 calories, 2 g fat, 1 g saturated fat, 9 mg cholesterol, 39 mg sodium

👑

LINDA'S DECADENT CHOCOLATE CAKE

Mom got this recipe many years ago from a coworker at the school district. The recipe card is discolored from so much use. The cake was low fat before low fat was popular. We ate it not because it was low fat, but because it was a moist and delicious chocolate cake. I revised it a bit to make it more low sodium friendly.

2 c. sugar or Splenda (or 1 c. sugar, 1 c. Splenda)
3 c. flour
2 t. soda
¼ t. salt
1/3 c. cocoa
2 c. cold water
¾ c. canola oil
2 T. vinegar (white or cider)
1 t. vanilla

Mix all together. Pour into 9x13 baking pan, sprayed with cooking spray. Bake 350 degrees for 30 to 40 minutes or until toothpick inserted in center comes out clean.

Frosting:
1 1/3 c. sugar
6 T. light tub margarine or unsalted butter
6 T. low fat milk

Boil above for 2 minutes. Turn off heat and add ½ c. dark chocolate chips. Beat until smooth and pour over cake. Yummy!

Per serving = 318 calories, 1 g saturated fat, 0 cholesterol, 20 mg sodium

LOW FAT LEMON BARS

Yummy lemon bars are a favorite of mine.

Crust:
¾ c. Splenda
¾ c. flour
Pinch of salt
¼ c. light butter
Filling:
2 T. flour
1 ¼ c. Splenda
½ c. egg substitute
½ c. fat free evaporated milk
½ c. lemon juice
1 T. grated lemon peel
¼ c. low sugar raspberry preserves

Crust: Mix Splenda, flour and salt, cut in light butter until crumbly – do not over mix. Press into baking pan. Bake 15 to 20 minutes until lightly browned.

Filling: Stir together flour and Splenda in bowl. Add egg substitute and evaporated milk. Stir until blended. Slowly add lemon juice while stirring constantly. Add lemon peel.

Stir the raspberry preserves and spread preserves over warm crust.

Gently pour lemon mix over the preserves.

Bake 20 to 25 minutes or until set. Allow to cool before placing in refrigerator. Chill at least 2 hours before serving. Sprinkle with powdered sugar prior to serving, if desired.

Per serving = 80 calories, 2.5 g fat, 1.5 g saturated fat, 10 mg cholesterol, 60 mg sodium

MOM'S APPLE CRISP

Easy recipe, and Mom always made it best!

6 large apples, peeled and chopped
1 ½ T. flour
1 c. sugar
1 t. cinnamon
¾ c. brown sugar
¾ c. oatmeal
¾ c. flour
¼ t. salt
1/3 c. light butter
¼ t. baking powder
¼ t. baking soda
¼ c. water

Mix first 4 ingredients and place in bottom of 9x13 pan that
has been coated with nonstick baking spray. Mix remaining
ingredients except water together. Crumble over apples.
Sprinkle ¼ c. water over top. Bake 350 degrees for one hour.

Per serving = 204 calories, 3 g saturated fat, 15 mg cholesterol, 89 mg sodium

MOM'S APPLE SQUARES

This is a bit of work, but is so yummy. This is one of those "okay for a splurge now and again" desserts. Mom's original recipe was changed to use a combination of whole wheat and all-purpose flour, less salt and unsalted butter. Still almost as good as the original. And I feel better eating the slimmed-down version.

1 ½ c. all-purpose flour
1 c. whole wheat flour
1 c. unsalted butter
½ t. salt
1 T. sugar

Mix above 5 ingredients like pie crust.

1 egg (separate yolk and white)
Low fat milk

Beat 1 egg yolk in a measuring cup and add enough low fat milk to make 2/3 c.

Add yolk and milk to the above pie crust mixture.

1 c. crushed corn flakes
8 apples, peeled and sliced
¾ c. sugar
1 t. cinnamon

Roll ½ of dough (pie crust plus egg yolk/milk) to fit jelly roll pan and cover the dough with crushed corn flakes. Arrange 8 or more peeled, sliced apples on the dough. Mix ¾ c. sugar (or combination of sugar and Splenda) with 1 t. cinnamon. Sprinkle sugar and cinnamon on top of the apples.

Roll out remaining half of dough for top crust and place on top of the apples. Seal edges, beat egg white and brush top of crust with egg white. Bake for 1 hour at 375 degrees.

Drizzle with powdered sugar icing or glaze.

Per serving = 235 calories, 2 g saturated fat, 19 mg cholesterol, 56 mg sodium

MOM'S PUMPKIN CHOCOLATE CHIP COOKIES

When my nephew Jack thinks about his favorite cookie made by Grandma Betty, this one immediately comes to mind. This is Mom's recipe with some minor revisions to lighten it up and lower sodium a bit.

1 ½ c. light margarine
2. c. light brown sugar
1 egg
1 (16 oz) can pumpkin (Mom always used Libby's)
4 c. flour
2 t. soda
2 t. cinnamon
½ t. salt
1 t. vanilla
1 ½ c. dark chocolate chips
2 c. quick oatmeal

Cream margarine and brown sugar. Add egg, and then add pumpkin. Combine dry ingredients and add to above mixture. Add vanilla and chocolate chips. Mix in oatmeal. (Mom used a wooden spoon, as the mixture is quite heavy. That and I burned out my old table mixer when I made the cookies many, many years ago!)

Bake 14 minutes in 350 degree oven. Frost, if desired, with cream cheese frosting (but we like them best plain).

Per serving (2 cookies) = 112 calories, 3 g saturated fat, 15 mg cholesterol, 68 mg sodium

OATMEAL RASPBERRY BARS

*Another good recipe from our friends at the Cardiac Rehab
Center at Essentia Health.*

1 ½ c. flour
1 t. baking powder
¼ t. salt
½ c. sugar
½ g. light brown sugar
½ c. light tub margarine
1 ½ c. quick oatmeal
2 containers fresh raspberries, crushed
1 c. low sugar raspberry jam
1 (3 oz) pkg. sugar free raspberry Jell-O
½ c. chopped pecans

Preheat oven to 350 degrees. Prepare a 9x12 baking pan with
nonstick baking spray.

In a large bowl, stir together flour, baking powder, salt and
sugars until blended. Cut in margarine until crumbly. Add
oatmeal and mix all together. Press about 2/3 of the mixture
into the bottom of the pan. Combine raspberries and jam;
spread over the crumb layer, pressing down lightly with the
back of a spoon. Sprinkle Jell-O over raspberry layer. Sprinkle
remaining crumbs over raspberries and Jell-O. Top with
chopped pecans.

Bake for 35 to 40 minutes or until lightly browned. Cool in pan.

Yield: 36 small bars

Per serving = 76 calories, .5 g saturated fat, 0 cholesterol, 45 mg sodium

OLD-FASHIONED MOLASSES CAKE

This is a no-frills, good cake. Tasty with nonfat whipped topping.

2 T. reduced fat butter or margarine, softened
¼ c. sugar
1 egg
½ c. molasses
1 c. flour
1 t. baking soda
¼ t. ginger
¼ t. cinnamon
1/8 t. allspice
1/8 t. salt
½ c. hot water
Fat free whipped topping

Beat butter or margarine and sugar in small bowl until crumbly. Add egg, then molasses, beating well. Combine flour, baking soda, spices and salt; add to butter mixture alternately with water.

Transfer to a 9 in. square baking pan coated with nonstick baking spray. Bake for 25 to 30 minutes at 350 degrees or until a toothpick inserted in the center comes out clean. Cut into squares; garnish with whipped topping.

Per serving (1 piece with 1 T. whipped topping) = 148 calories, 1 g saturated fat, 28 mg cholesterol, 205 mg sodium

PUMPKIN ROLL

*Original recipe came from my good friend Deb. Sooooo good.
I just had to skinny it up a bit, and it still tastes sooooo good.
Thanks Deb! (One can of pumpkin is enough for 2 pumpkin
rolls—you can always freeze one).*

Blend
3 eggs
1 c. sugar
2/3 c. pumpkin (1/2 can)
Add
2/3 c. flour
1 t. soda
1 heaping t. pumpkin spice

Mix and spread on a well-greased (otherwise it sticks) jelly roll pan.
Bake at 370 degrees (yup, that's 370) for about 12 minutes. When
cake is done, immediately turn onto damp tea towel on counter and
roll up in the towel from narrow end to cool 5 to 10 minutes.

Make filling:
1 c. powdered sugar
8 oz. reduced fat cream cheese
4 T. light tub margarine (or reduced fat butter)
1 ½ t. vanilla

Unroll cake, spread on filling and carefully roll up again.
Refrigerate. Second roll, if it lasts that long, can be frozen for up
to 4 months. Thaw in refrigerator.

Per serving = 140 calories, 1 g saturated fat, 81 mg cholesterol, 249 mg sodium

WESTHAVEN BARS

My mom often made these when I was a kid. I continue to make them, a bit revised from the original recipe that came from a well-used church cookbook. Cocoa makes them lower fat, and they don't need any frosting!

1 c. dates cut fine
1 c. boiling water
1 t. soda
½ c. unsalted butter
1 c. sugar (or ½ c. sugar, ½ c. Splenda)
2 eggs (or equivalent egg substitute)
1 ½ c. flour
2 heaping T. cocoa
¼ t. salt
1 pkg. dark chocolate chips
Chopped walnuts

Add dates to boiling water, add soda and cool. Cream butter and sugar, add eggs one at a time, and then add cooled dates and water mixture. Add dry ingredients and put in a 9x13 pan (coated with nonstick baking spray). Sprinkle with chocolate chips and chopped walnuts. Bake at 350 degrees for 30 minutes or until toothpick inserted in center of cake comes out clean.

Per serving = 195 calories, 1 g saturated fat, 18 mg cholesterol, 145 mg sodium

ZUCCHINI CHOCOLATE CAKE

This cake is a combined recipe from my friend Karen's mom, Carol, and Essentia's Cardiac Rehab Center.

¾ c. sugar
¾ c. Splenda
½ c. canola oil
½ c. light tub margarine
2 t. vanilla extract
1 t. almond extract
2 eggs
½ c. buttermilk
1 ½ c whole wheat flour
1 c. all-purpose flour
4 heaping T. cocoa powder
½ t. baking powder
1 t. baking soda
2 c. grated (unpeeled) zucchini
½ c. chopped dates
½ c. chopped walnuts

Preheat oven to 350 degrees. Prepare a 9x13 pan with nonstick baking spray. Mix sugar and Splenda, oil, margarine, extracts, eggs, and buttermilk together. Add dry ingredients and mix well. Fold in grated zucchini and chopped dates. Pour into pan. Sprinkle nuts over top. Bake for 35 minutes.

Another variation: Omit cocoa powder, increase vanilla to 3 t. Add dates, walnuts and raisins (1/2 c. each) to batter. Bake 30 to 35 minutes or until toothpick inserted in center comes out clean.

Per serving = 175 calories, 3 g fat, 1 g saturated fat, 20 mg cholesterol, 80 mg sodium

INDEX OF RECIPES

A

Almond Shortbread Thumbprints 150
Almost Giada's Turkey Meatballs 90
Amish Roast 92
Amore Italian Chicken 93
Apple Cranberry Crisp 151
Apple Pancakes 28
Aunt Elaine's Pepper Steak 95

B

Baked Basil Wedges 76
Baked Orange Chicken 96
Banana Oatmeal Bread 22
Beef Barley Soup 46
Betty's Sukiyaki 98
BOUNTIFUL BREAKFASTS 27 - 36
BREAD MACHINE RECIPES 15 - 20
Breakfast Sausage 29
Breakfast Scramble 30
Breakfast Tacos 31

C

Caesar Dressing 66
Caramel Sauce 159
Cherry Cobbler Crumble 152
Cherry Oat Squares 153
Chewy Oatmeal Drop Cookies 154
Chicken Barley Soup 47
Chicken Caprese 99
Chicken Manicotti 100
Chicken Rice and Broccoli Bake 102
Chicken Wild Rice Soup 48
Chicken with Cocoa Tomato Sauce 104
Chicken/Turkey A La King 106
Chili 49
Chili Tortilla Bake 107

Chocolate Chip Banana Bread 24
Chocolate Oatmeal Cake 155
Cindy's Meatloaf 109
Cinnamon Cranberry Oat Energy Bars 156
Company Mashed Taters 77
Condensed Cream of Mushroom Soup 50
Cooking Show Tomato Sauce 91
Cranberry Cake 158
Cranberry Chicken 110
Cranberry Cole Slaw 67
Cranberry Nut Biscotti 160
Cream Soup Mix Substitute 51
Crockpot Beans 78
Crockpot Chicken Cacciatore 111

D

Dark Chocolate Raspberry Cake 162
Dark Chocolate Sauce 164

E

East Low Fat Coleslaw 68
Easy Chocolate Frosting 166
Egg Substitutes 43
Extraordinary White Bread 16

F

Family Goulash 112
Fat Free Dill Dip 4
Fat-Free Chocolate Therapy Cake 165
Favorite Brown Beef Stew 52
Fluffy Key Lime Pie 167
French Bread 17
Fresh Apple Dump Cake 168
Fruit Pizza 170
Fruity Coleslaw 69

G

Garlic-Dill Smashed Potatoes 79
**GATHER AROUND THE
DINNER TABLE** 89 - 147
Grape Tomato Bruschetta 5
Ground Beef and Vegetable Soup 53
Guacamole 6

H

Hannah's Banana Bread 25
Herbed Stew with Heat 54
"Hidden Valley" Ranch Dressing Mix 38
Honey Wheat Bread 18

I

Italian Bread 19
Italian Sausage 113

J

JUST FOR STARTERS 3 - 12

K

Key Lime Dip 7

L

Lightened-up Holiday Cookie Dough 172
Linda's Decadent Chocolate Cake 174
Low Fat Lemon Bars 175
Low Fat Lemon Blueberry Loaf 26
Low Sodium BBQ Sauce 39
Lush Lettuce Salad 70

M

Major League Manicotti 114
MAKE IT A SAVORY SIDE 75 - 88
Meatballs for Mom's Spaghetti 121
Meatloaf with Tomato Sauce 116
Mexican Lasagna 117

Minestrone Soup 56
Mom's Apple Crisp 177
Mom's Apple Squares 178
Mom's Chop Suey 119
Mom's Famous Spaghetti 120
Mom's Holiday Brunch 32
Mom's Pumpkin Chocolate Chip Cookies 180
Multigrain Bread 20

O

Oatmeal Raspberry Bars 181
Old-Fashioned Molasses Cake 183
Oregano Lemon Chicken 122
Orzo Skillet 123
Oven Baked Chicken Tenders 124
Oven Baked Fajitas 125

P

Pancakes 34
Parmesan Pecan Chicken 126
Parsley Smashed Potatoes 80
Party Crunch Mix 8
Pasta Pizza Soup 58
Pizza Sauce 127
Polynesian Meatballs 128
Pumpkin Roll 184

Q

QUICK BREADS 21 - 26

R

Red Lentil Soup 59
Refrigerator Sweet Pickles 40
Roasted Vegetables 81
Roasted Zucchini 82

S

Savory Potato Salad 71
Scalloped Corn 83
Simple Scalloped Potatoes (Microwave) 84
Sloppy Joes Two 132
Sloppy Joes with Red Lentils 130
Slow Cooker Cajun Chicken Breasts 133
Slow Cooker Cranberry Pork 134
Southwest Chipotle Pork Chops 135
Southwestern Pulled Pork 137
Soy Sauce Substitute 41
Spinach Salad with Oranges 72
SPRINKLE LIBERALLY WITH CONDIMENTS .... 37 - 43
Strawberry Spinach Salad I 73
Strawberry Spinach Salad II 74
SWEET ENDINGS .... 149 - 187
Swiss Scalloped Potatoes 85

T

Taco Casserole 138
Taco Seasoning 42
Tex Mex Pork Chops 139
THE SMELL OF GOOD BREAD BAKING .... 13 - 20
Three Grain Pilaf 87
Tomato Basil Soup 60
Tortilla Roll Ups 9
TOSS ME A SALAD .... 65 - 74
Turkey Black Bean Chili 61
Twice Baked Potatoes 88

U

Uncle Dick's Lasagna 143
Upside Down Pizza 140
**USE YOUR SPOON: SUSTAINING
SOUPS AND STEWS** 45 - 63

V

Vanilla Walnut Crunchies 10
Vegetable Beef Soup 63
Vegetable Lasagna 145
Vegetable Pizza with Cauliflower Crust 141
Veggie Egg Strata 35
Veggie Pinwheel Appetizers 11
Veggie Pizza 12

W

Westhaven Bars 185
White House Turkey Lasagna with
Spinach—Revised 146
Whole Wheat Waffles 36

Z

Zucchini Chocolate Cake 186

About The Author

Cindy Stratioti is a lifelong Duluthian. Aside from healthy cooking and baking, she enjoys traveling, gardening, reading, shopping and whatever the day brings. She enjoys all of the pleasures of an unstructured life. She is a proud wife, mother, sister, aunt and friend.

Author and her husband Jeff, posing with his American Heart Association Lifestyle Change Award in 2013.

41235560R00125

Made in the USA
Charleston, SC
22 April 2015